Learning throughout life: challenges for the twenty-first century

Learning throughout life: challenges for the twenty-first century

Education on the move

UNESCO PUBLISHING

The authors are responsible for the choice and the
presentation of the facts contained in this book and
for the opinions expressed therein which are not
necessarily those of UNESCO and do not commit
the Organization.

The designations employed and the presentation
of material throughout this publication do not imply
the expression of any opinion whatsoever on the
part of UNESCO concerning the legal status of any
country, territory, city or area or of its authorities, or
concerning the delimitation of its frontiers or
boundaries.

Published in 2002 by the United Nations
Educational, Scientific and Cultural Organization,
7, place de Fontenoy,
75352 Paris 07 SP (France)

Typeset by Marina Rubio, 93200, Saint-Denis
Printed by Imprimerie CORLET, Z.I., route de Vire,
F-14110, Condé-sur-Noireau - (57548)

ISBN 92-3-103812-5

Printed in France

Foreword

The International Commission on Education for the Twenty-first Century, under the chairmanship of Jacques Delors, reported back to UNESCO in April 1996 after three years of reflection. Its report, *Learning: The Treasure Within*, revolved around the essential theme of learning throughout life. Widely debated within the educational community and in political circles and used in a number of countries as the springboard for discussions about the nature and future of educational reform, the report has had a major influence on UNESCO's education programme. At the request of the Director-General of UNESCO, Jacques Delors agreed to preside over a task force to ensure continuity within the follow-up to the Commission's reflections and recommendations.

It is in this context that a conference on learning throughout life was organized in Lisbon, 8–9 March 1999, by UNESCO and the Calouste Gulbenkian Foundation. At a time of dramatic changes in the economic and societal structures of the world, learning throughout life is not a luxury but a necessity. Yet, as the following chapters make clear, the conference realized that learning throughout life remains largely a noble aim, and that the recognition of learning acquisition was very largely the monopoly of formal education. This book is an attempt to clarify some of the issues involved in making learning throughout life a reality for everyone, especially the traditionally dispossessed.

Learning throughout Life – Twenty-first Century Challenges brings together in English the proceedings of the Lisbon meeting. It is intended for educationalists and policy-makers concerned with ensuring the availability of opportunities for learning throughout life in both formal and non-formal contexts.

UNESCO would like to express its appreciation to Jacques Delors for his vital role in both the follow-up of *Learning: The Treasure Within* and the Lisbon meeting. Thanks are also due to the Calouste Gulbenkian Foundation and to the participants who contributed to this publication: Maria Teresa Ambrósio, Roberto Carneiro, Felicity Everiss, María de Ibarrola, Abdul W. Khan, Toby Linden, Enver Motala, George Papadopoulos and Francesc Pedró.

Contents

Introduction

Karen MacGregor
South African journalist
and foreign correspondent
for international newspapers,
specializing in
education and politics

At the dawn of the new millennium, there is global consensus on the need for lifelong learning. Governments agree that it is the key to economic prosperity and to the development of societies in a rapidly changing, technologically advancing world. But there are other equally important imperatives powering the global drive towards learning throughout life, and these include the need to build better relationships between people, groups and nations, for greater equity and for personal development – the wish for all people, as Jacques Delors put it in his seminal report, to unlock 'the treasure within'.

While learning throughout life as an idea has been globally accepted, strategies needed to support this philosophical commitment have been patchily applied in most countries. Furthermore, it is a broad and evolving concept that can mean different things to different groups in different cultures, so there is little consensus on how best to proceed along the road to lifelong learning. In many less developed nations, still under enormous pressure to provide universal primary or secondary education, the resources needed to design and implement appropriate lifelong learning opportunities are scarce or simply not there.

A major challenge for the twenty-first century is to capture the spirit and rhetoric of lifelong learning and the notion of a 'learning society', and to translate these into achievable and effective policies and practices. By so doing it may be possible to unleash new opportunities for learning that could power human development globally and ultimately move the world closer to the ideals of human rights, peace, freedom and social justice.

It is with these goals in mind – as well as taking forward foundational work already done in the area of learning throughout life by UNESCO and its International Commission on Education for the Twenty-first Century – that this report was conceived and written.

In March 1999, a team of educational experts from around the world gathered in Lisbon to discuss issues around lifelong learning and, crucially, ways of progressing towards it. The meeting was hosted jointly by the Calouste Gulbenkian Foundation in Lisbon, Portugal's National Board of Education and UNESCO. This report draws on papers and talks presented at the conference, and a round table discussion that concluded it.

The Delors report

In 1991, the General Conference of UNESCO proposed creating an International Commission on Education for the Twenty-first Century, to reflect on the future of education and learning. Jacques Delors, the former European Commission president, was invited to chair a panel of fourteen distinguished specialists from around the world and from a range of cultures and professions.[1] The Commission was financed and supported by UNESCO but is independent in its work.

Drawing on UNESCO's resources, international experience and previous studies, the panel spent three years identifying lines of inquiry and themes, studying literature and consulting with experts from a range of professions, organizations and states. Its 1996 report, *Learning: The Treasure Within*, has had a significant impact globally on discussions about learning; it has inspired a large number of meetings and generated editions in many languages.

Education and lifelong learning, argued the Commission, are about more than improving knowledge and skills; they are at the heart of personal and social development. In confronting future challenges, education could also be an exceptional means of building relations

1. Members of the Commission were: Jacques Delors (France, Chairman); In'am Al Mufti (Jordan); Isao Amagi (Japan); Roberto Carneiro (Portugal); Fay Chung (Zimbabwe); Bronislaw Geremek (Poland); William Gorham (United States); Aleksandra Kornhauser (Slovenia); Michael Manley (Jamaica); Marisela Padrón Quero (Venezuela); Marie-Angélique Savané (Senegal); Karan Singh (India); Rodolfo Stavenhagen (Mexico); Myong Won Suhr (Republic of Korea); Zhou Nanzhao (China).

between people, groups and nations, and of attaining the ideals upon which UNESCO was founded – human rights, peace, freedom and social justice. As Jacques Delors wrote: 'The Commission does not see education as a miracle cure or a magic formula opening the door to a world in which all ideals will be attained, but as one of the principal means available to foster a deeper and more harmonious form of human development and thereby to reduce poverty, exclusion, ignorance, oppression and war.'[2]

The report built on four pillars it identified as constituting the foundations of education, to provide a framework for how societies might move towards learning throughout life – which was a focus of the Commission – and a 'necessary Utopia' in which all people's talents (the treasure that lies buried within them) are realized. The four pillars are:

- Learning to know – broad general education with possible in-depth study of selected subjects, to provide a 'passport' to lifelong education by laying educational foundations and giving people a taste for lifelong learning.
- Learning to do – learning to do a job of work and acquiring competence to deal with a variety of situations and to work in teams. This can sometimes best be acquired by involving pupils and students in work experience and social schemes.
- Learning to live together – learning to understand others and their history, traditions and spiritual values, the aim being to encourage people to implement common projects and to manage conflicts intelligently and peacefully: a necessary Utopia, wrote Delors, if we are to escape a currently dangerous cycle sustained by cynicism and resignation.
- Learning to be – the theme of Edgar Faure's report *Learning to Be*,[3] which called for combining greater independence and judgement with strong personal responsibility to attain common goals. The

2. Jacques Delors, 'Education: The Necessary Utopia', in J. Delors et al., *Learning: The Treasure Within; Report to UNESCO of the International Commission on Education for the Twenty-first Century*, pp. 13–35, Paris, UNESCO Publishing, 1996.
3. Edgar Faure et al., *Learning to Be: The World of Education Today and Tomorrow*, Paris/London, UNESCO/Harrap, 1972.

Commission stressed a further imperative: that none of the talents that lie within every individual must be left untapped.

The Commission's ideas thus went far beyond mere educational reform. While reasserting the vital need for basic education, it also stressed the pivotal role of secondary education in the learning processes of young people and in social development. The central role of teachers and the need to improve their training, status and working conditions was emphasized, as was the use of technology in the service of education through adequate training for later use at work and in daily life. Tertiary institutions should be not only centres of knowledge and professional training but also crossroads for lifelong learning and international co-operation.

The focus of *Learning: The Treasure Within* on lifelong learning thus did not imply less reflection on different levels of education: rather, it called for a fresh approach to the learning process, based on more flexible education systems in which people's opportunities and values are enhanced. Lifelong learning and creating a 'learning society' were seen as far broader than merely strengthening adult education opportunities, as they are sometimes interpreted to be.

Despite remarkable scientific and economic development in many countries in the twentieth century, the Commission pointed out, disillusionment accompanied progress. This is manifested in widening inequalities within and between countries, growing threats to the environment, continued conflict worldwide and apathy towards democracy in many rich countries. It also highlighted major tensions that are central to the problems of the twenty-first century between the global and the local, the universal and the individual, tradition and modernity, long-term and short-term considerations, the need for competition and concern for equality of opportunity, the expansion of knowledge and people's capacity to assimilate it, and the spiritual and the material.

Education must face up to such problems 'now more than ever as a world society struggles painfully to be born',[4] as it is at the heart of personal and community development and has a crucial contribution to make towards building a better world. The Commission felt that lifelong learning, with its advantages of flexibility, diversity and avail-

4. Delors, op. cit., p. 19.

ability at different times and in different places, would significantly expand opportunities for human development:

> There is a need to rethink and broaden the notion of lifelong education. Not only must it adapt to changes in the nature of work, but it must also constitute a continuous process of forming whole human beings – their knowledge and aptitudes, as well as critical faculty and the ability to act. It should enable people to develop awareness of themselves and their environment and encourage them to play their social role at work and in the community.[5]

The concept of learning throughout life is key to the twenty-first century, the Commission argued, reaching beyond traditional distinctions between initial and continuing education and helping to meet challenges posed by a rapidly changing world. This is not a new insight, but the need for education to enable people to deal with new situations arising in their personal and working lives is growing stronger, and it requires people to learn how to learn. Changes in traditional ways of life also demand better understanding of other people and the world, which is why the Commission stressed 'Learning to Live Together'.

Such an approach, it added, does not detract from the definition of basic learning needs produced at the 1990 World Conference on Education for All in Jomtien, Thailand: the needs required by all people to survive, develop their full potential, live and work in dignity, participate in development, improve the quality of their lives, make informed decisions and continue learning.[6] But good basic education should be combined with out-of-school approaches that enable people to experience the three dimensions of education – ethical and cultural, scientific and technological, and economic and social – to learn about themselves, develop interpersonal skills, and acquire basic knowledge and skills.

The Commission was convinced that diversification of types of study made easily available would help make the most of all forms of

5.   Ibid, p. 21.
6.   World Conference on Education for All, 5–9 March 1990, Jomtien, Thailand. World Declaration on Education for All. New York, Inter-Agency Commission for WCEFA, 1990, Art. 1, para. 1.

talent, reducing academic failure and the exclusion from learning and society of many young people. Conventional education should combine with approaches that alternate learning with work experience, with bridges between them to correct errors in choice of direction. The prospect of going back to study would also assure young people that their fate is not sealed forever by the age of 20 years. Higher education too should strive to avoid excluding young people, and diversify what it offers.

> Quite simply, learning throughout life makes it possible to organize the various stages of education to provide for passage from one stage to another and to diversify the paths through the system, while enhancing the value of each. This could be a way of avoiding the invidious choice between selection by ability, which increases the number of academic failures and the risks of exclusion, and the same education for all, which can inhibit talent.[7]

Learning: The Treasure Within emphasized the need for a long-term approach if reforms are to succeed, and for incremental, achievable change that involves the main parties key to the success of educational reform – local communities, public authorities and the international community. Attempts to impose educational reforms from the top down, or from outside, are doomed to failure; consultation is essential and the Commission urged cautious decentralization to increase local responsibility for and involvement in education, and scope for innovation.

Since no reform can succeed without the co-operation and participation of teachers, the Commission recommended that the status of educators be considered a matter of priority, that the content of teacher training be altered, and that teachers be given access to continuing education. It also called for education systems to be provided with well-trained teachers and the resources needed to deliver quality education, and for teachers to work in teams in order to achieve flexibility in courses and provide academic and career guidance with a view to lifelong learning.

Improving education, the Commission argued, requires policy makers to face responsibility and not leave it to market forces or self-

7. Delors, op. cit., p. 24.

regulation to put things right when they go wrong. Public authorities must propose clear options, consult broadly, choose policies that chart the way ahead and regulate their education systems through adjustments. Education is a public good: once this principle is accepted, public and private funding may be combined in ways that take into account traditions, stages of development, ways of life and income distribution – with all choices predicated on the fundamental principle of equality of opportunity.

International organizations, which are increasingly called on to find solutions to problems with a global dimension but achieve largely inadequate results, need to reform themselves to make their action more effective. Among other things, the Commission proposed allocating at least a quarter of development aid to education, creating 'debt for education swaps' to offset adverse effects of adjustment policies, introducing information technologies in all countries to ease the growing gap between the rich and poor worlds, and working with grassroots non-governmental organizations to support international co-operation – with such actions seen as partnerships between developed and developing countries rather than as aid.

Learning throughout life – new perspectives

Learning: The Treasure Within was the starting point of the Lisbon conference, which then proceeded to examine learning throughout life in greater detail, exploring theoretical and educational issues, the development of the concept and progress achieved as well as new ways of teaching, the role of new technologies and country experiences. Presentations were divided into three themes – milestones along the road to lifelong learning, teaching beyond the boundaries of formal education, and country responses to the need for lifelong earning. This book is arranged into three similar sections, and concluded by Jacques Delors.

Milestones along the road to lifelong learning

In Chapter 1, George Papadopoulos, former OECD deputy director of education, overviews international trends in lifelong learning policies, outlining new features of current approaches, presenting the work of major international organizations active in the field, and providing examples of country practices. He mentions four major challenges that must be met if the rhetoric of lifelong learning is to become reality.

First, developing a culture of lifelong learning has to be motivated by more than an economic rationale. Policies directed at raising participation across all groups need to make lifelong learning attractive to the individual and a satisfaction in itself. This requires radically changing the ethos of foundation education, transforming the teaching/learning process in schools and eradicating failure. Without progress in this area, those who are deprived of initial education will remain those who do not benefit from continuing education opportunities.

Second, the persistent gap between general and vocational education and training – a phenomenon of societies that attach greater value to theoretical than to practical knowledge – needs to be bridged.

Third, employers need to become more involved in lifelong learning, increasing their contribution so as to gain collectively from the benefits of a learning society.

Finally, there is the affordability of implementing lifelong-learning policies, especially if the fight against social exclusion is taken seriously. New resources are needed and can only marginally be found by switching funds from other sectors of education or applying efficiency and cost-reducing measures in delivering lifelong learning. Public funding needs to be supplemented by increased contributions from individuals and employers, if lifelong learning is to become a reality.

> Under such circumstances, implementing lifelong learning policies can only be done incrementally, and this is what is already happening in a number of countries. The challenge is to ensure that an incremental approach is planned and implemented within an agreed framework for the long term realization of lifelong learning.

Roberto Carneiro of Portugal, editor in chief of the *Journal of Education and Society*, sketches the new frontiers of education in Chapter 2 and refers to three trends providing the context for education development this century: the interplay between globalization and the search for roots; the quest for social cohesion, inclusion and increased democracy; and the transition from inequitable economic growth to sustainable human development. These require far-reaching changes in the way educational priorities are cast.

The concept of knowledge societies is heralded as the new mainstream paradigm, with knowledge driving development and new growth theories inspired by the contribution of knowledge to technological innovation. Not surprisingly, this has propelled education to the centre stage of strategic thinking and developed learning into a kind of post-modern ideology and consensual agenda for the future, laying the basis for a new social contract: education is not only a right but also a moral duty and an integral part of citizenship and social activity.

Knowledge is expanding rapidly and mutating constantly, the most important change being from objective to subjective knowledge which is a personal construct and intensely social. Lifelong-learning strategies need to adapt to new knowledge patterns, and to move from objective to constructive knowledge, from an industrial to a learning society, from instruction to personal learning, from communication to knowledge acquisition, and from schooling to non-formal modes of learning.

There has been a conceptual shift in thinking away from traditional school as the dominant mode of delivery towards multiple modes in which learning can occur in the same place or in different places, at the same time or at different times, which is in line with the requirements of a knowledge-based society. To make the most of this philosophy, 'knowing to know' will have to shift from a strictly Western 'rational' canon of knowledge, which is unable fully to interpret a complex, uncertain world, to a global canon, which is open to the best epistemic contributions of all cultures and to the advantages of diversity.

In Chapter 3, Professor Maria Teresa Ambrósio, President of the National Council of Education in Portugal, outlines challenges thrown up by lifelong learning, which she presents as a new approach to learning – a wider route to be taken by people of all ages in all of education and training's different locations and situations, and a process for constructing the individual and for permanently acquiring knowledge that refers to the social, cultural and economic pillars of which adults are part.

Learning how to learn is a specific challenge in today's information society, and is about 'how to seek information, analyse it, use it and change it daily into knowledge', though this should not be separated from holistic social, cultural and ethical dimensions of learning. The change in concept from school learning to ongoing learning that is the individual's response to society is extremely important and arises with emergence of a new type of pupil, a 'social individual who learns' and is immersed in a dynamic society that trains her/him.

Profound change and the challenges of lifelong learning require us to rethink the education we have and to invent new processes, systems and policies, because current systems do not stand up to the demands of lifelong learning. Achieving lifelong learning's goals will require multiple activities in the formal and informal education sectors, revising the socio-education contract on which current systems are based, the active involvement of both state and non-state actors, and many changes at the chalk face.

Developing countries have made great progress in education in the past three decades, writes Toby Linden, a knowledge co-ordinator at the World Bank, in Chapter 4. But they still face major problems on four fronts: (a) faltering access to education; (b) unequal access; (c) problems with poor quality, which wastes resources and drives people out of education; and (d) weak institutional capacity. Such problems place developing countries at a disadvantage in moving towards to a learning society, and growing populations will place even more pressure on their stressed, poorly resourced systems.

Nevertheless, lifelong learning is a relevant goal for developing countries, because: (a) labour is more efficient with the application of knowledge; (b) all countries need a flexible work force; (c) many developing nations in any case have advanced education systems; and (d) in all countries the undereducated face declining prospects. Global changes demand that less developed countries reform their education systems, and it makes sense to do so within a policy framework of lifelong learning which would also help improve education access and quality.

Countries everywhere still use traditional teaching practices. This gives hope to developing countries, because in this sense at least they are at the same stage as many rich nations. Indeed, some of the innovations needed to make lifelong learning a reality are to be found in developing countries: many have leveraged resources through private education systems; some have already experimented with creative incentive, voucher and tax credit schemes; and many have long experience in using technology to encourage learners and reach otherwise excluded populations. Developing countries also have a history of community-based learning.

Lifelong learning: necessary in a changing world

Felicity Everiss, formerly of the Department for Education and Employment in the United Kingdom, looks in Chapter 5 at the experiences of England, a country that has travelled further down the road to lifelong learning than most others.

A range of new policies has been introduced, aimed at encouraging learning 'from the cradle to the grave', starting with improved early childhood provision and support for parental learning. There are policies to improve quality in schools, state intervention in unsuccessful schools and 'education action zones' introducing innovative learning into areas with low performance, public–private partnerships and strong stress on excellent teaching.

There are also policies aimed at widening participation in post-compulsory learning and providing more opportunities for more groups. Programmes are being created for youngsters outside the formal tertiary system such as apprenticeships, time off for study, education maintenance allowances, career guidance and a 'New Deal' for the young unemployed. Companies are being encouraged to invest in their employees through lifelong learning and a system of national standards is being created to ensure the quality of, and recognition for, workplace learning.

Further and higher education institutions are working to improve access, especially for non-traditional groups. A 'University for Industry' is being created to link learners to opportunities, promote lifelong learning and ensure that institutions respond to people's needs. A telephone helpline provides information on opportunities, 'local learning centres' are being created and new materials are being produced to broaden opportunities and use information technologies to support learning. Finally, 'learning accounts' are being created offering financial credit for learning, providing incentives to learn and supporting learning for people in work.

But there are many challenges in implementing lifelong learning strategies. There is a need to change people's attitudes to investing in learning and to achieve a fair funding balance between formal, informal and work based learning. To justify investment it is necessary, but often difficult, to demonstrate rates of return. Institutions that have been encouraged to compete now need to share resources and collaborate. And finally, in England there are issues around national control of education and the growing development of 'bottom-up' activity that responds to the needs of local people and areas.

Teaching in a new perspective

Universities have a key role to play in creating a learning society, but have not fully exploited opportunities opened up by new technologies to change the way people teach and learn, writes Professor Francesc Pedró of Spain's Universitat Pompeu Fabra in Chapter 6. Even universities whose students use the Internet widely continue to employ traditional models, with technology added on with varying degrees of success. If higher education is to train professionals fully able to participate in a learning society, it needs to introduce information technology into all subjects and contexts so that it becomes an automatic tool in learning, and to change its teaching practices.

Educational renewal will require universities to: (a) provide all-round training to lay the basis for lifelong learning while preparing students for high-level occupations; (b) review content and method; (c) combine theoretical grounding with problem solving and project development; (d) impart communication, co-operative and information handling skills; (e) shift the focus from teachers to students; and (f) accept a wide variety of students. All this will require vocational training for lecturers, adequate funding and institutional change.

The use of new technologies will open the way for educational innovation. A good example is the virtual campuses that have sprung up around the world and can be defined as learning networks that use digital technology as a connecting medium. One great advantage of virtual campuses is that, using the Internet, students can access learning materials at any time and place, use electronic management and payment, and communicate easily with teachers and fellow students – in short, have permanent access to education in ways not possible before.

New technologies also make it possible to revisit what high-quality education is. They provide access to a large volume of information, multimedia and instant communication, making it possible to rethink what goes on in the lecture room. Freed of time spent on verbal teaching, lecturers could in future focus more on the work of each student and on developing quality learning materials, for instance. Problems range from the need for infrastructure and a technologically competent population to acceptance by teachers. But by combining the advantages of traditional and virtual campuses, it may be possible for universities to improve access to and quality of higher education worldwide – and help create a learning society.

In Chapter 7, Professor María de Ibarrola of the Instituto Politécnico Nacional in Mexico argues that the rapid changes of recent decades – globalization, technological progress and political and cultural transformation – demand new and ever higher levels of knowledge, literacy, skills and practices. Strong basic education is the critical provider of such skills, but despite profound educational reforms most Latin American countries still have high illiteracy rates, low education levels, and school systems that are unequal and insufficient for major population groups. Adult education is mostly oriented towards literacy and primary schooling; more appealing learning opportunities are difficult to find and on the job training is rare.

There are sharply different and unequal points of departure for large population sectors and these determine their potential to benefit from lifelong learning. Millions of young people are effectively excluded from education and work in Latin America, secondary schooling has been neglected, those who profit most from lifelong learning tend to be the already well educated and countries have been largely unable to exploit new technologies.

Despite all this, most Latin American countries have had lifelong learning policies for decades, with professional updating through universities a visible example. What is new is realization of the need for constantly changing competences and for lifelong learning for all – an ideal that must start with basic schooling. Countries need to direct resources towards new basic-school opportunities as well as flexible, accessible lifelong learning that answers a multiplicity of needs, recognizes different kinds of learning and consolidates institutions.

Lifelong learning is a public matter and cannot be left to a market dynamic that stresses either the demand or supply of learning opportunities. But an interesting mix of public–private interaction is emerging, with new social actors and new ways of developing policies and programmes that involve both public and private entities. At the global level, international co-operation has to take fully into consideration the fact that lifelong learning policies in countries where basic education needs have long been satisfied cannot be exported without perverse effects to countries where basic schooling for all is still but a distant dream.

South African education consultant Enver Motala points out in Chapter 8 that most experience of lifelong learning has been obtained in stable societies. But very different problems face countries in transition, among them particular development challenges, high popular expectations combined with lack of resources, and globalization's undermining of the nation-state, which in poor countries is the only mechanism available to protect sovereignty, overcome deficits and encourage even development.

Since the country's transition to democracy in 1994, South Africa's new government has produced an array of excellent policies tackling fundamental problems such as equity, redress, access, quality and relevance in every sphere. Policy documents reflect the need for flexible learning systems, there are strategies to encourage lifelong learning and institutions have been set up to implement them. But the task of delivering reform is enormous. South Africa remains one of the most unequal societies in the world, and the school system is poorly funded, racked by conflict, and lacking essential infrastructure and resources.

There are broader problems. Economic determinism pervades the language of education, which is constantly criticized and judged by narrow measures that speak little about the sociological or humanistic imperatives that drive educational policy change. Spending on education is directly related to fiscal targets, which means there is little left over after expenditure on staff for buildings and books, let alone new technologies.

External pressures on macro-economic and fiscal policies are restricting the state from using its power to fulfil its responsibilities or intervene in market failures. International agencies committed to democracy and social justice, such as UNESCO, could provide a bulwark against the predatory instincts of powerful interests that determine the fate of nations. Strong international agencies and their interventions, linked to critical national responses, might be the only way to hold back the tide of oppressive global divisions.

Finally, in Chapter 9, Professor Abdul W. Khan, then Vice-chancellor of India's Indira Gandhi National Open University and now Assistant Director-General for Communication and Information at UNESCO, argues that open and distance learning is ideally suited to lifelong learning and indeed arose in response to the same needs for greater access, equity and opportunity.

Open and distance learning transmits education programmes to individuals and groups separated in space and/or time. This requires a process that is centred on the learner and encourages learner autonomy, which in turn improves access to learning. There are wide choices in courses and combinations, and mobility between institutions through credit-transfer mechanisms, which also contributes to learner autonomy. Further, the stress is on course delivery through multiple channels – direct to learners, through resource centres and extension activities – via multiple means ranging from print and audiovisual cassettes to broadcast programmes, computer networks and facilitators.

New information and communication technologies are central to open and distance learning and are used to overcome socio-economic barriers and communication gaps, to improve access and flexibility, to enhance virtual proximity and interactivity, and to offer a variety of learning resources, thereby enabling individualized learning and providing powerful cognitive tools.

Open and distance learning have powered extraordinary growth in the number and types of learners, and today there are a wide range of types of providers and trends towards multi-mode institutions and collaborative approaches. There are also greater breadth in operations and a growing diversity of programmes, and moves towards multimedia, a greater variety of learning resources, as well as more interactive technologies and extension activities.

Challenges ahead

Despite almost universal recognition of its value, the road to learning throughout life is long and difficult everywhere. The very concept means different things to different people, may need to be thought of as a cluster of ideas and definitely needs to be better understood and developed. Although the Delors report identified the need for lifelong learning and painted a picture of the destination towards which education systems ought to be heading, there is great uncertainty about exactly how best to proceed and what the priorities should be.

A strong connection has been made between lifelong learning and economic development, with this link one of the imperatives driving government interest in learning throughout life. In education and training circles, it is believed more importantly to be key to personal and community development. These approaches are not necessarily mutually exclusive: as the Delors Commission took pains to point out, learning throughout life can encourage development in all sorts of ways – economically as well as in terms of personal development, quality of life and building relationships between people, groups and countries.

There are many theories about how to encourage lifelong learning and many excellent examples of how this has been done – from using information technology and the Internet in Spain to creating an open university in India to public–private projects in Latin America. Nevertheless, there are daunting obstacles along the path towards lifelong learning, and big differences within and between countries in terms of what is needed and the problems to be faced.

Globalization – referring to strong trends towards reduced trade barriers, greater capital flows and the communication revolution, which are transcending national boundaries – for instance, is having an impact on all countries and on the development of lifelong learning. But globalization can be seen in many ways and consists of multiple tendencies which affect countries variously. Within countries, globalization's impact differs in different local contexts.

During the round-table discussion at the end of the Lisbon conference, delegates grappled with such issues in an effort to identify major challenges ahead for lifelong learning and possible ways of tackling them. The conference itself represented one way forward, which is to share experience and best practice at the international level.

At the discourse level, all countries have the same dream of a learning society in which everyone enrols in a learning 'spiral' that enables them fully to participate in society and the economy. But no country is able to say that it provides sufficient basic education for everybody, and there are enormous differences between countries in the resources and institutions available to move from discourse to practice. As María de Ibarrola stated: 'We all have the same need for lifelong education and we are all pursuing general values like diversity, democracy, respect for differences and cultural plurality. But we have very different departure points and vastly different needs. Perhaps, then, the development of lifelong education will have to be an explosion of all sorts of activities.'

Jacques Delors raised four challenges that need to be addressed if efforts to promote lifelong learning are to succeed in the coming years:

- Policy makers, education actors and client groups in all countries need to be convinced of the need for education throughout life.
- Ways must be found to manage successful transitions from current education systems to ones conducive to learning throughout life.
- There is a need to study clusters of countries facing similar

challenges, analysing their evolutions, contexts and best practices so as to discover the particular types of problems they face in promoting lifelong learning and what their different solutions might be.

- International organizations must consult and co-operate with each other, and encourage information sharing among countries, to stimulate worldwide progress in lifelong learning.

The need for lifelong learning

Learning: The Treasure Within presented powerful arguments in favour of lifelong learning. It is a goal assumed worthy by the Lisbon conference and this report, not seen in terms of trade-offs – economic versus human, primary versus secondary education and so on – but as an overarching prospect with win-win developmental potential.

The purpose here is not to restate the case for lifelong learning, but to explore ways of promoting the concept. There are problems with developing and implementing lifelong learning strategies when there is intense competition from entrenched educational interests or other priorities, or lack of resources generally, or people have limited opportunities, lack of foundational learning or are excluded from existing education systems.

Knowledge, says Roberto Carneiro, is seen as the engine of development and learning as its fuel. The World Bank is evolving a knowledge-for-development plan while, for the rich world, economic growth is based on knowledge-driven societies. This hard notion of knowledge as a production or development factor creeps into strategies. But if learning throughout life is to become a truly common goal, it needs to be alluring to the individual, the satisfaction itself as people strive to become better and learning becomes seen as a path to happiness and self-construction, and not just a development tool. Lifelong learning needs to empower people through a multiplicity of learning opportunities that enable them to improve the quality of their lives, combining the notions of choice and responsibility:

> The message of lifelong learning is that the intrinsic value of education sustains the economic return: the message that needs to be sold is that investment in education launches a virtuous circle whereby education contributes not only to economic well-being but also to spiritual and social well-being, and that it creates the

economic resources to sustain further investment in education, further advancement and well-being.

People should indeed come to care about learning and to be happier for it, argues Toby Linden, and in this regard there is much to learn from business-labour initiatives that have negotiated innovative lifelong learning packages that go way beyond work requirements. But other incentives – such as education aimed at obtaining a job – should also be used to 'sell' the concept. European surveys have shown that what unemployed people want most is a job, and part of young people's disaffection from education is that they do not see it as providing skills or leading to a job. If this is correct, then education systems are failing to find out what people's abilities are and to provide an appropriate learning response.

The many reasons for lifelong learning need to be articulated and actively promoted in ways that make sense to politicians and people, or lifelong learning will not become central to policy agendas. International organizations should continue their work on the good returns of investing in education, choosing their words carefully so as not to seem threatening to each other. Economists need to see lifelong learning as crucial to growth and development, and educationists to see economic inputs as supporting the cause of education, if both are to line up solidly behind lifelong learning efforts.

Transitions to lifelong learning

Education systems have evolved over centuries and the way they are organized has come to be seen as set in stone. But lifelong learning requires radical reforms to, *inter alia*, link formal and informal education, and increase access to learning opportunities. Roberto Carneiro identifies four major issues to be tackled when thinking about lifelong learning strategies: (a) market imperfections and the need for public policies; (b) exclusion from education systems; (c) the demands of new knowledge; and (d) lack of international dialogue.

Market imperfections have been clearly identified in lifelong learning. For example, supply and demand need to be reconciled. Not all people are aware of their needs and there is often lack of information needed to make informed choices. Also, there are market failures in the sustainable financing and provision of lifelong learning (which public–private partnerships could help resolve). There is clear market failure in the recognition and accreditation of non-formal competences in countries that only value formal qualifications. A host of policies is needed in most countries to tackle such problems. Many also need to regulate quality, to develop fiscal policies such as subsidies to finance lifelong learning and to redistribute funding.

A second issue is the cumulative exclusion that comes with lifelong learning. There is plenty of evidence that a first generation of exclusion occurs in schools and, since learning generates more learning, this ratchets up education systems until lifelong learning becomes the preserve of the well educated. Problems of access, participation and quality in schooling have to be solved because that is where the foundations for lifelong learning are laid.

It is likely that different lifelong learning strategies are needed for people excluded during basic education, rather than the same strategies for all; that some positive discrimination is required in which excluded groups are clearly targeted; and that much stronger components of citizenship and democracy have to be built into lifelong learning strategies, steering away from a strictly utilitarian approach to link lifelong learning to lifelong citizenship.

A third question is about 'new learning', under whose umbrella falls all new knowledge, teaching and learning methods, and the role of new technologies and multimedia in learning. This is about providing creative authoring tools, databases and training for teachers to develop their own materials. It is about finding ways of combining theoretical and practical knowledge, codified and tacit knowledge, institutional and corporate curricula, ways of learning by doing, and ways of learning in diverse and multicultural contexts.

Finally, most countries still know little of what is happening elsewhere but they need this knowledge if they are to avoid reinventing the wheel as they grapple with lifelong-learning issues. There needs to be more sharing of experience between countries and identification of best practice.

Further, says Carneiro, policy makers and education actors need to look carefully at new tensions such as that between learning for competitiveness and learning for co-operation. As economies and societies change, communities are being confronted with problems – new markets, joblessness, reorganization of work, etc. – that demand collaborative efforts and knowledge-sharing if they are to adapt and survive. Another growing tension is between formal and non-formal education, with the latter usually referring to adult education outside the formal school and tertiary system. Formal institutions often supply 'non-formal' learning, but there are many activities that are self-organized or provided by groups, companies and non-profit organizations, that strategies for lifelong learning ought to encompass.

George Papadopoulos highlights two other tensions that need to be resolved. The first is between educationists who consider themselves guardians of quality, and those outside the profession who influence education policy and practice, such as politicians and administrators. Another tension is not as much between tradition and modernity as between modernity and post-modernity. Modernity is already here, but post-modernity calls for reforms and for revolutionizing development; it is a major new consideration.

Such broad issues are essential to laying the groundwork for strategies aimed at education reform. Ultimately, however, countries need to decide priorities within an achievable strategic framework so that structured decisions can be made, policies and market failures can be measured and new policy interventions targeted. Carneiro proposes three public policies that could have an impact on institutional change: study time entitlements after schooling to stimulate demand for lifelong learning; placing teachers at the centre of learning and investing heavily in their retraining and resourcing with new authoring tools; and a dual system of learning that bridges humanities and professional studies.

The Delors report reflected on the need to break with old paradigms and look at new ways of learning. The role of teachers is probably going to change, while partnerships between states, civil society organizations and the private sector are increasingly seen as supporting and changing educational efforts. Seen in the context of an evolving knowledge society, lifelong learning is a multidimensional effort involving diverse itineraries – continuing learning opportunities, use of new technologies and the Internet, community participation, antidotes to unlearning and so on – that will set the scene and pace for profound reform.

Different problems, different solutions

The need to set priorities and policy frameworks becomes starkly clear when lifelong learning is looked at from an international perspective.

Different societies face different challenges in developing and applying appropriate strategies. Vastly disparate levels of education and resources between advanced and developing countries are just two cases in point, with less developed countries lacking the resources even to achieve solid basic education.

Ten years after the end of the Cold War and a global embrace of democracy and the market, says Enver Motala, there is still a lot to be understood about the world's societies in transition, and how they should develop and cope with major demands on the state. Change needs to be managed and experience of transition so far is that it must be incremental: key targets must be identified rather than an attempt to solve all problems at once. Globalization has eroded the role of states, while market forces have been unable to ensure equitable development. All this has a profound impact on what lifelong learning can hope to achieve.

Further problems with implementing lifelong learning in developing countries, according to Abdul W. Kahn, are lack of co-ordination and the inappropriate use of technologies. Even in countries with well-developed proposals, for example on how to use technology to enhance learning opportunities for communities, development agencies have embarked on projects that make no reference to those policies. Gaps between what is articulated and what is practised regularly result in policy exercises going to waste.

Many people, including those in countries with strong education systems, do not have access to quality learning; many are not committed to learning; and many slip through the formal education net to become marginalized from the economy and society. And within countries, such as Australia with its aboriginal people, there are cultures at different points of transition. Ways need to be found to offer such groups better access to quality learning that respects their culture while also enabling them to enjoy living in a wider society.

There is much evidence of increasing inequalities between developed and developing countries, and within countries between the privileged and disadvantaged. But ways of correcting this growing imbalance have yet to be found. María de Ibarrola argues that states need to focus on different learning strategies because of their different departure points. Developing nations have the least resources but the greatest need for a variety of programmes, or gaps will continue to widen between them and the advanced world:

In developing countries, where there are wide disparities between rich and poor, we need to focus on many programmes, give them the same priority and resource them by creating more democratic distribution of wealth through key public policies and partnerships. It is an awesome task.

Learning is a social product and is not culture free. A first step in reform is thus to understand how learning takes place in a particular cultural and historical context. All cultures have specific ways of nurturing learning and every education system is the outcome of struggles that include a diversity of cultures. If we understand those, it may be possible, with the help of international organizations, to conduct comparative studies that help cultures build their own aims and strategies.

The role of international organizations

Most countries know little of what is happening regarding lifelong learning elsewhere. An international perspective reveals the extent of differences between countries, and starts to uncover what the lifelong learning picture looks like as a whole and what ideals to pursue. The Lisbon conference agreed that there is a need to share experience, identify best practice and set benchmarks that enable countries and the global community to measure progress in lifelong learning. International organizations need systematically to showcase what is happening, in publications, at fairs and at conferences.

Promoting the need for lifelong learning

In persuading people of the need for lifelong learning, said Alexandra Draxler, Secretary of the International Commission for Education in the Twenty-first Century, international agencies could usefully help marshal convincing evidence – for policy makers because they release funds, for education actors because they have to put lifelong learning in place, and for clients because demand is simply not there among many target populations and is not likely to be unless incentives are introduced. While there is economic evidence of the value of lifelong learning, this is not yet true for less tangible areas such as civic and personal development.

It could also be useful to find out why people become detached from education and society: the reasons may or may not be country specific. UNESCO studies, for instance, show that two major factors are poverty – in developing countries especially, parents cannot afford to keep children in school – and poor quality, which is linked to poverty. There are likely to be several reasons why adults do not return to education, including their perceptions of its utility and lack of opportunity, which are pertinent to lifelong learning efforts.

For groups of people excluded from education (those who realize they need knowledge and skills as well as alienated people who see no future for themselves), country experiences could be helpful in discovering ways of creating opportunities for people to improve their knowledge, skills and life chances based on their particular circumstances and needs.

Since demand for lifelong learning is often not there, says Roberto Carneiro, international agencies should actively promote the concept on the global stage. An alliance of agencies could study marketing lessons from global groups like Microsoft and Nike, develop an interesting 'brand' for lifelong learning and work with the media to promote the idea – in ways that respect local cultures but arrive, via different routes, at the same destination.

People attach different meanings to lifelong learning, and there is often lack of clarity about what the term refers to. This confusion is perpetuated in major documents of international organizations: the Council of Europe is concerned with enlarging European citizenship, focusing on democratic values and European identity, the European Commission and the Organisation for Economic Co-operation and Development (OECD) stress economic and technological dynamics and needs, while UNESCO sees learning as a means of improving life chances. International organizations ought to build bridges between these different approaches to construct a coherent picture of lifelong learning.

Transitions to lifelong learning

While advanced economies are engaging with questions of how to institute lifelong learning, this makes less sense in countries still trying to guarantee foundational learning – or indeed for excluded groups in developed countries. But a knowledge society can only seek moral justification on the grounds of greater equity. This presents a conundrum, according to OECD Deputy Director of Education, Barry McGaw: people most in need of lifelong learning, on whom opportunities should primarily be focused, are those who have little foundational education and are least able to take up opportunities.

A key policy question is how to redistribute lifelong learning resources in ways that help the disadvantaged. It may be necessary to tax people upon whom substantial educational funds have already been spent, and to direct shared public resources towards people who have not yet reaped the benefits. Countries with free tertiary systems have found that the middle classes benefit the most, with their higher-education participation cross-subsidized by working class families. Without redistributive funding mechanisms, there is a risk that the same thing will happen with lifelong learning. At the international level, redistribution of resources for lifelong learning could be pursued through debt swaps for education, exchange of scientists and researchers, and earmarking a quarter of aid for education, says Carneiro.

Information technologies have a key role to play in lifelong learning and a learning society, according to Francesc Pedró. International organizations could be helpful, first, in promoting research on the appropriate uses and widespread acceptance of new technologies and, second, in helping countries, institutions and communities to net-work across boundaries. Finally, they could help policy makers and educators to promote integrated policies: lifelong learning via techno-logy, requires infrastructural development and the collaboration of many state sectors.

International co-operation has a fundamental role to play in the comparative analysis of lifelong learning and the dissemination of information and analysis. Developing countries especially need to be researched, according to former UNESCO Deputy Director-General for Education, Colin Power. For instance, there is a great deal of evidence that literacy and skills programmes for women are highly constructive, especially when linked to improved opportunities. It is necessary to look more at the particular life circumstances of the dis-advantaged and discover what empowers them, at how to create links between what learners need and the education they receive, and at how to provide learning incentives – and to promote and actively support initiatives.

Problems facing developing countries need to be the concern of international agencies and groups like the World Bank and European Union that are able to support development. In efforts to promote learning in developing countries and marginalized groups everywhere, the international community needs to build new relationships with governments at all levels and to vigorously support policy development at global and national levels, and lifelong learning programmes at community level. But the first obligation of international co-operation, says María de Ibarrola, should be to respect the potential of each country and provide knowledge of what is happening elsewhere.

Different problems, different solutions

Since lifelong learning priorities and actions are largely determined by a country's stage of development, argues George Papadopoulos, future research could identify groups of countries at similar stages of development or with similar problems, and focus on how they are tackling lifelong learning. Counties participating in international studies could offer input on their problems, policies and practical measures, leading to discussion about learning in various contexts. International organizations should pragmatically focus on gathering and analysing collective wisdom and experience.

Organizations could also collaborate on research by focusing on different subsets of their member countries, using similar methodologies and frameworks to gather information that could be shared. An example is the OECD study of lifelong learning in twenty-nine countries which has looked *inter alia* at new forms of finance. It would be strategically useful for UNESCO to look at other subsets among its Member States in a similar study, and for the two organizations to pool and analyse their results.

To set up a dialogue between countries at different stages of development, Enver Motala considers it necessary to look at several characteristics to see how they can be clustered. Historical and contextual conditions must be key in determining clusters or the discourse might be disempowering. Developing countries make the mistake of using the experiences of developed nations to inform new policies. But models of success in one country may not work in another, if the starting points are very different and the problems to be resolved do not connect with the solutions proposed. Policy makers need to use appropriate exemplars.

Another way of clustering countries could be by first identifying the learning challenges they face and focusing on how they go about tackling them, or by identifying strands common to particular experiences, possibly citing some countries as examples of different groups. It may not be necessary to cluster countries at the outset of research: a sensible approach could be to draw in countries willing and able to participate, and let typologies emerge at a later stage.

Indeed, international organizations are sometimes accused of wasting scarce resources in poor countries by asking them to produce information that is of limited use to them. It is important not to add to the administrative burden of countries if it means that they cannot attend to their own needs. However, as Alexandra Draxler suggested, it is feasible to draw on academic groups in countries, who are best qualified to conduct studies and usually keen to do so – where possible under an international co-ordinator who could help to set study indicators while leaving countries free to investigate issues of relevance to them.

Researchers generally measure what they know how to measure and therefore tend to study individual learning, looking at how people turn learning into marketable knowledge. But if learning to live together is to be taken seriously, then learning in groups needs to be better understood. Western experts who advise developing countries may fail to offer workable solutions because they do not focus on group learning, which is important in many countries but is not the way of Western education systems. International organizations might usefully facilitate research that investigates different kinds of learning and takes forward the 'learning to live together' concept that was central to *Learning: The Treasure Within*.

Part one
Where are we? Milestones along the road to lifelong learning

1. Policies for lifelong learning: an overview of international trends

George Papadopoulos
Former Deputy Director
of Education at the OECD

Consecration of the concept of lifelong learning was a remarkable phenomenon in the international discourse on education during the decade of the 1990s. Even more remarkable has been widespread acceptance that strategies for lifelong learning will provide the panacea to many of the problems – economic, social, cultural and even political – confronting societies as they enter the twenty-first century.

Both the rationale and the objectives of policies for lifelong learning have been amply stated (and advocated) in the work of international organizations, in official policy statements by governments, and in the rapidly growing volume of specialized literature in this field.

What should be underlined is the gap between acceptance of the concept and its practical application as policy. It has happened before: governments find it easy to endorse concepts and principles of drastic educational change, only to find that their practical application becomes thwarted by lack of new resources and the corporatist behaviour of the established system, buttressed by vested interests, including political ideologies.

There is a real danger that this may already be happening with lifelong learning. The alacrity with which governments have endorsed the concept is, with certain exceptions, only palely reflected in concrete and consistent measures of implementation, let alone the institution of overall strategies. So much so that there is a clear tendency in many countries to place under the umbrella of lifelong learning all the disparate initiatives that have been introduced in different parts of their education and training systems, and that can be interpreted as responding in some way to the objectives of lifelong learning. Similarly, and as a result of this ad hoc approach, there is a marked tendency in many countries for the lifelong learning concept to be hijacked by lobbies – traditional adult education, community and popular education groups, vocational training and apprenticeship institutions, entrenched schooling protagonists, universities and other tertiary institutions – in order to secure additional resources and political support for their own aggrandisement.

With these considerations in mind, this chapter, drawing on international experience, is designed to: (a) outline a number of general features characteristic of the current approach to lifelong learning as distinguished from earlier approaches; (b) present the work of major international organizations – the Council of Europe, UNESCO, the OECD and the European Union – that have been active in this field, have helped define the rationale and objectives of lifelong learning, and have stimulated its practical acceptance and implementation in individual countries; provide examples of actual country practices and experience in terms of both overall strategies and thematic experimentation; and suggest, in conclusion, the lessons that can be drawn from this experience so far, in terms of bottlenecks to be overcome and prospects for the future.

The current approach to lifelong learning

The concept of lifelong learning is not new. In a sense, it goes back to Plato and Aristotle, even though in those remote days the main concern was with the continuing education of individuals to enable them to perform their role as active citizens – as 'political animals', in the Aristotelian definition of man. This remains an important objective of education to the present day and it is significant that the 'popular education' and 'workers' education' movements that originated in Scandinavia and spread throughout Europe in the nineteenth century had cultural, social and, indirectly, political rather than directly work-related goals as their primary objectives (Kallen, 1996). These aims remained prevalent even after the rapid expansion and institutionalization of adult education, and it was only after the Second World War that the need for organized retraining of workers and links to the formal education system began seriously to be recognized.

It was in this new climate, propelled by rapidly increasing social and economic demands and the massive expansion of education, that from the 1960s new models for providing education began to emerge under such titles as 'recurrent education', 'continuing education and training' and *'education permanente'*, with lifelong learning as their leitmotif. The title of the 1973 OECD publication, *Recurrent Education: A Strategy for Lifelong Learning*, speaks for itself.

This brief incursion into history enables us to see how the antecedents of lifelong learning have been shaped by changing socio-economic and political conditions. It is in this changed context that the distinctive features of policies for lifelong learning can be identified.

First, it is important to note that whereas previous paradigms were primarily driven by initially cultural and then social (particularly equal opportunities) objectives, the driving forces behind the current advocacy of lifelong learning are economic-cum-technological imperatives and needs arising from increasingly knowledge- and information-based economies operating in a competitive globalized market system. True, broad objectives such as social cohesion, cultural and democratic values, etc. are taken into account. But these are subsumed as products of an economy revitalized through lifelong learning rather than as prime movers of the strategy.

Second, and a clear reflection of the point made above, lifelong learning policies have received more weighty political support than previously, when political endorsement was limited at best to education ministers. Within the OECD, for example, the precepts of policies for 'lifelong learning for all' were endorsed not only by ministers of education, but also by ministers of employment, of social affairs and, finally, ministers of finance. This augurs well for the availability of additional resources for lifelong learning ventures, and is a reflection of the wider social and economic objectives of lifelong learning.

Third, previously recurrent or permanent education was conceived essentially in the context of formal education. The coverage is now much broader, to encompass all learning activity wherever it takes place, including enterprise-based training and individual learning, especially through new technologies. Indeed, the emphasis is on the learner and his or her needs and the propagation of self-directed learning. The imaginative use of information technologies is an integral part of strategies for lifelong learning.

Finally, a word of caution. 'Learning' is a vital part of the educational process, but it is not synonymous with 'education'. There is a danger that lifelong learning will be narrowly interpreted to imply the mere mastery of specific bits of knowledge or skills. This danger is reinforced by the economic-technological impetus behind the concept – reflected in the emphasis that present policies for lifelong learning place on training – as well as by the current trend to base judgements of educational achievement on aspects amenable to quantitative measurement. Lifelong learning strategies need to ensure that their objectives go well beyond this narrow, instrumental definition of learning. This is particularly relevant to the training component of strategies which continues, by and large, to be treated in isolation from the humanistic culture of which it should be an integral part.

The perspectives of international organizations

In retrospect it is interesting to note that the concept of lifelong learning, which as we have seen had its origins in the 1960s, surfaced almost simultaneously in three major international organizations – the Council of Europe, UNESCO and the OECD. Although each had its own focal points of interest and action in this area, according to their respective missions and membership, the central idea was the same: the development of coherent strategies for the provision of education and training opportunities for all individuals over their whole life-span.

Over time, this idea came to permeate all the educational activities of the three organizations. However, in the case of the Council of Europe and UNESCO, it would be true to say that the tendency has been for the concept to be diluted within the more traditional sectors of education, whereas in the OECD and recently the European Union, there has been a more consistent and aggressive approach, both analytically and in terms of policy formation and implementation.

The Council of Europe

Initiated in the early 1960s, the concept of *'education permanente'* became the hallmark of Council of Europe educational activities throughout that decade and the next (Council of Europe, 1970, 1977, 1978). It was propagated as a 'fundamentally new and comprehensive concept ... an overall educational pattern capable of meeting the rapidly increasing and ever more diversified educational needs of every individual, young and adult, in the new European society' (Council of Europe, 1970). It was seen as the best strategy for promoting equal educational opportunity; but a strategy that would need to be organized with the full agreement and participation of all parties concerned, and one that would bring together theory and practice, knowledge and competence, learning and doing (Council of Europe, 1978; Kallen, 1996).

Over the years, these principles gained widespread acceptance in member countries and no doubt gave credence to a number of piece-meal programmes. Essentially, however, they remained locked in established sectoral programmes of formal education and, apart from generating a climate of opinion in favour of lifelong learning, they had little impact on the development of a coherent strategy as implied in the original concept.

UNESCO

Unlike the other three organizations, with their regional and rather homogeneous constituencies, UNESCO is confronted with an almost impossible task in putting forward a comprehensive educational policy concept that gives unity to its new programmes and meets the widely different needs, interests and priorities of its worldwide members. Its entry into the arena of lifelong learning was consequently a slow and cautious process inspired largely by insights gained through its activities, during the 1950s and 1960s, in the field of adult education – themselves a response to the pressing problem of reducing adult illiteracy in developing countries. This culminated in 1970 in the publication of UNESCO's first report on lifelong learning (Lengrand, 1970), followed by the creation of the International Commission on the Development of Education under the chairmanship of Edgar Faure. The Commission's report was published under the alluring title *Learning to Be: The World of Education Today and Tomorrow* (Faure et al., 1972).

In its advocacy of the importance of lifelong learning, based on the individual's innate desire to learn and thereby leading to a more humane society, the report was welcomed by the whole of the UNESCO membership, irrespective of levels of development and political affiliations. On the whole, it would be true to say that *Learning to Be*, couched as it was in general and conceptual terms, served more as a source of inspiration than a guide to practical action. Its impact on opinion should not be underestimated; nor should the stimulus it gave to launching specific programmes related to the concept of lifelong learning, particularly literacy and adult education programmes. On the whole, however, neither in countries nor within UNESCO itself were the precepts of the report translated into global approaches to educational policies (Kallen, 1996).

One generation after *Learning to Be* the exercise was repeated, along almost identical lines. This time an International Commission, chaired by Jacques Delors, was charged with reporting on 'Education for the Twenty-first Century' – a weighty assignment matched by the title of the resulting report *Learning: The Treasure Within* (Delors, 1996). Compared with its predecessor, the Delors report, while fully endorsing the humanistic values and objectives of education, represents some significant departures in its analysis of problems and proposals for their solution in line with the changed socio-economic and political context in which education now operates – particularly the impact of globalization, technology and increasingly knowledge-based economies.

Identifying the four pillars that are the foundations of education – learning to be, learning to know, learning to do and learning to live together – the report advocates policies for lifelong learning ('the heartbeat of society') much more explicitly than did its predecessor, as the only way forward. It stresses the need for a fresh approach:

> to the stages and bridges of learning, whereby the paths through education systems become more varied and the value of each is enhanced. While universal basic education is an absolute priority, secondary education has a pivotal role to play in the individual learning paths of young people and in the development of societies. And, higher education institutions should be diversified so as to take into account their functions and duties as centres of knowledge, as places of professional training, as the cross-roads for learning throughout life and as partners in international co-operation ... in a world increasingly dominated by technology, emphasis must be placed on ways both to use technology in the service of education and to prepare people to master it for living and working. Getting the reform strategies right, by a broad-based dialogue, and by increasing responsibility and involvement of stakeholders at every level, will be a crucial element of educational renewal. (Delors, 1996).

As with its predecessor, the Delors report has been generally endorsed and has given rise to much discussion within individual countries and in regional conferences. It remains to be seen what its direct impact on policies, and on the education programmes of UNESCO itself, will be.

The OECD

Activities relating to lifelong learning have been a regular feature of OECD programmes over the last three decades. They have been fully analysed and documented, reflecting the organization's special approach to education and training policies in relating them to other sectors, particularly social and economic policies (Papadopoulos, 1994). In these relations, lifelong learning has provided a continuous, unifying theme, with the emphasis shifting over time between the social and the economic rationale, according to the prevailing political climate concerning overall policy objectives.

Thus it was that during the affluent 1960s and early 1970s, when the main concern was with social objectives, particularly greater equality of opportunity, the OECD launched its Recurrent Education strategy (OECD, 1973), which it sustained for over a decade. Central to the strategy was spreading educational opportunities over the individual's lifetime, to be available when needed rather than concentrated in an ever lengthening period of initial and often ineffective education. Not the least merit of such a strategy would be the possibility of bringing together initial formal education and adult and on-the-job training into a single framework, thus enabling education and training to be attuned to the real needs of both the labour market and individuals. Over the longer term, applying such a strategy would require drastic changes to the organization of post-compulsory education, to allow for alternations between education, training and work with a guaranteed return to formal education when and for whom it was needed.

Considerable work was undertaken within the OECD, supported by member countries, in analysing the various facets and practical implications of recurrent education. Successive conferences of European ministers of education during the 1970s gave their full endorsement to the principles of such a strategy. And yet, in terms of application, such progress as was made remained piecemeal and unevenly spread across countries. Countries were ready to apply, and in fact did apply, individual features of recurrent education – particularly improving the status of vocational education and its link to general education, the transition of young people to working life, introducing schemes to encourage on-the-job training (such as paid educational leave) and improved access by adults to higher education. But in the end no country could muster the political will, or stamina, to embark on the radical changes to its established education systems that were called for by the new strategy.[1]

Current OECD work on lifelong learning is in many respects a continuation – but also a significant extension – of the recurrent education paradigm. At their 1990 meeting, OECD ministers of education concentrated their attention on the need to improve the quality of education at all levels and for all in society (OECD, 1992). The subject of their 1995 meeting was 'Making Lifelong Learning a Reality for All' (OECD, 1996). The shift in emphasis between meetings was significant. While the central objective, high-quality education and training for all, remained the same, the concern in 1996 was with how to give reality to this objective – the answer being by adopting strategies for lifelong learning as the organizing principle for guiding education and training policies, and introducing practical measures to give effect to such strategies.

That the ministers meant business, both in their own work and that of OECD, is well reflected in their communiqué.[2]

> We are all convinced of the crucial importance of learning through-out life for enriching personal lives, fostering economic growth and maintaining social cohesion, and we have agreed on strategies to implement it. OECD societies have made great strides during the 1990s, but now we need to find more effective ways of offering every one of our citizens such an opportunity. The target may be ambitious, but we cannot afford not to work towards it.

Stressing that strategies for lifelong learning need 'a whole-hearted commitment to new system-wide goals, standards and approaches', the communiqué identified four key issues crucial to the successful realization of such strategies. These are: (a) strengthening the foun-dations for learning throughout life by improving access to early childhood education, revitalizing schools and supporting the growth of

1. For a complete account of the recurrent education venture, and related bibliography, see Papadopoulos, 1994, pp. 112 *et seq.*
2. Introduction to the communiqué by the chairman, Simon Crean, Minister for Employment, Education and Training, Australia (OECD, 1996).

other formal and non-formal learning arrangements; (b) promoting coherent links between learning and work by establishing pathways and bridges that facilitate more flexible movement between education-training and work, and by improving the mechanisms for assessing and recognizing the skills and competences of individuals, whether acquired through formal or non-formal learning; (c) rethinking the role and responsibilities of all partners, including governments, who provide opportunities for learning; and (d) creating incentives – for individuals, employers and other education and training providers – to mobilize greater investment in lifelong learning opportunities. In each of these areas, the communiqué spells out in fair detail the nature of the problems that arise and of action needed to resolve them. Taken together, they amount to a blueprint for the implementation of strategies for lifelong learning. It should be compulsory reading for all those involved in such strategies (OECD, 1996, pp. 21–4).

In addition to action at the national level, the communiqué prescribes specific supporting activities for the OECD itself, ranging from technical and analytical work in the four areas and exchange of country experience to overall monitoring of progress towards realizing lifelong learning. The lifelong-learning approach now provides the unifying principle for all the educational activities of the organization, and their relationship to broader activities in the social, employment and economic sectors, responding to the need to develop stronger, more coherent partnerships between a wide range of actors across society. It is this consistent approach, brought about by the lifelong-learning imperative, that gives the OECD's work in education its new look.

The volume and variety of these activities precludes detailing them here. But there are three things of interest to note: first, the forward-looking approach to traditional education sectors, for example combating school failure, 'schools for tomorrow', teachers for tomorrow's schools, opening pathways from education to work and redefining tertiary education; second, advances made in monitoring country progress, particularly in the evolution of overall policies, of youth pathways and the financing of lifelong learning (OECD, 1998*a*); and third, analysis of the contribution of lifelong learning to broader social and economic issues, such as social exclusion, cities as learning centres and the development of internationally comparable indicators of adult literacy and human capital investment (OECD, 1998*b*). Some of these activities will be described, as they relate to the very active participation of member countries in them – a clear indication of the impact of OECD work on national situations.

The European Union

The European Union is not, of course, an international organization in the sense of the three other organizations. Its executive body, the Commission, is in fact the nearest thing to an international government that has been devised so far in the process of European integration. This gives it an advantage over other international agencies in that its remit is more prescriptive, its membership more concentrated and its resources more ample, enabling the Commission to mount large-scale projects in countries backed by substantial financial incentives and the political commitments that go with Union membership.

Education is not new to the European Union. What is new is the strategic importance it has now come to occupy in the broader social, employment and economic objectives of Union policies. Since the 1960s, under the restrictive mandate of the Treaty of Rome, action in education and training focused on co-operation, exchange of experience, support for innovation, and the development and co-ordination of training policies. It also boosted industry—education co-operation and the mobility of students and people in training. The turning point came in 1993, with the adoption of the *White Paper on Growth, Competitiveness and Employment*, which stressed that the development of education and training is one of the conditions for a new model of more employment-intensive growth. Coupled with increasing consensus within the Union on the need to increase and consolidate educational activity, the 1993 White Paper led to two new initiatives: setting out, in the form of guidelines for action, detailed proposals designed to serve as a basis for the Commission's policy in education and training – presented in a new *White Paper on Teaching and Learning: Towards the Learning Society* (1995); and the decision by the Council of Ministers and the European Parliament (October 1995) to designate 1996 the European Year of Lifelong Learning.

Both initiatives were aimed at provoking debate at every level on the need for lifelong learning, in order to 'sensitize Europeans to the upheavals brought about by the advent of the information society, the process of internationalization and scientific and technical progress, and to the potential contribution of education and training towards meeting this challenge' (Cresson, 1996).

Thus, the Union set itself on the road to lifelong learning, an objective which was incorporated in the Amsterdam Treaty expressing determination to promote high levels of knowledge through broad access to education and its permanent updating. The stage was set for the final act – guidelines for future European Union action in the areas of education, training and youth for the period 2000 to 2006, presented in the 1997 *White Paper: Towards a Europe of Knowledge* (European Union, 1997).

It is interesting to note, in looking at the evolution of European Union commitment to lifelong learning, that there has been a shift (to many people, a welcome shift) from the initial heavily economic rationale to one that takes on social concerns as well. This is clearly observed in the differences between the 1995 and the 1997 White Papers.

In the former, *Towards the Learning Society*, the societal impact of the three challenges (information, internationalization, and scientific and technological knowledge) was seen in terms of changes in working patterns, job creation, production methods and competitiveness. The overall response was believed to lie in reinforcing the merits of a broad base of knowledge and in building up employability, all couched in language that to many of its critics was reminiscent of the familiar perspective of technological determinism (D'Iribane, 1996).

The gist of the White Paper was in its guidelines for action, which were to shape European Union work over the next two years. These were grouped under the following five general objectives: (a) encouraging the acquisition of new knowledge – recognition of skills; mobility; multimedia educational software; (b) bringing schools and the business sector closer together – apprenticeship-trainee schemes and vocational training; (c) combating exclusion – second-chance school and European voluntary service; (d) ensuring proficiency in three community languages; and (e) treating capital investment and investment in training on an equal basis.

The pursuit of these objectives was propagated and tested out in the massive programme of activities organized during the European Year of Lifelong Learning. More than 500 events were held at all levels in the form of conferences, seminars, competitions, multimedia development work, the designing and dissemination of educational software, television programmes and the publication of examples of good practice, covering all forms of formal and non-formal education and training. National co-ordinating bodies were appointed by member states to direct projects at national, regional and local level, disseminate information and contribute to assessment and follow-up in their countries. On the basis of this collective experience, in December 1996 the European Union Council adopted conclusions on lifelong learning which influenced the guidelines for future European Union action put forward in *Towards a Europe of Knowledge* (European Union, 1997).

The shift in emphasis from the earlier paper is evident in two respects. First, it reflects the explicit recognition given to the importance of knowledge policies which the Commission had already put forward as one of the four fundamental pillars of Union policies:

> Real wealth creation will henceforward be linked to the production and dissemination of knowledge and will depend first and foremost on new efforts in the field of research, education and training and our capacity to promote innovation. This is why we must fashion a veritable 'Europe of Knowledge'. This process is directly linked to the aim of developing lifelong learning.

Second, it recognizes that the contribution of learning to community development and social inclusion, to fostering a sense of citizenship, responsibility and identity, is as important as its contribution to the economy.

> We must try to bridge the 'learning divide' – between those who have benefited from education and training and those who have not. Thus, the social dimension of education and its role in the enhancement of citizenship have now joined knowledge and employability as the three dimensions for . . . the gradual construction of an open and dynamic European educational area.

To move in this direction, six types of action are envisaged: physical mobility, extending to all target groups; virtual mobility, mobility through communication and information networks, and the production and dissemination of multimedia and audiovisual products and services; building co-operation networks at European level to facilitate exchange of experience and good practice; promoting language skills and understanding of different cultures; pursuing innovation through pilot projects based on transnational partnerships to create education and training products or instruments for the accreditation of skills; and improving community sources of reference with regard to education, training and youth systems and policies in member states – for example, databases and knowledge of education systems.

Essential to the success of activities in these areas is creating a framework of responsibilities shared between the community, member states and other partners – educational, social, economic, regional and local, and partners in the voluntary sector. Developing such partnerships, both in the design and delivery of lifelong-learning programmes, is increasingly seen as a necessary condition for the success of programmes.

Country experience

There can be no doubting that the work of international organizations has stimulated, supported and helped legitimize lifelong learning work undertaken in countries, at government as well as local and institutional levels. But while it has been fairly easy to sketch out a rational and coherent approach at the international level, it is more difficult to do the same when it comes to the plethora of national programmes initiated in many countries under the banner of lifelong learning.

However, the significance of these programmes should not be underestimated. Mostly, they are targeted at specific population groups or problem areas within country-specific contexts. In a few cases – Finland, the Netherlands, Norway, Sweden and the United Kingdom, for example – they are presented as integral parts of national strategies for lifelong learning. Together they reflect a quasi-universal *prise de conscience* on the part of national governments of the importance of lifelong learning as the ultimate objective for the long-term development of education and training policies, always seen as essential to their social and economic prosperity. This is clearly reflected in the evidence made available to the OECD as part of its ongoing monitoring of the implementation of lifelong learning policies in member countries.

Based on this evidence, representative examples of country experience are presented below.

Overall policies

Few countries have enunciated overall policies for lifelong learning that are accompanied by implementable measures. These are embodied in official publications, of which only summary indications can be given here.

A good example is provided by England in its Green Paper *The Learning Age: A Renaissance for a New Britain*, submitted to Parliament in February 1998 (parallel documents were issued for Scotland and Wales). The ambitious targets set out in the paper include: priority for an extra 500,000 people in further and higher education by 2002; doubling help for basic literacy and numeracy skills among adults, to involve more than 500,000 adults a year by 2002; providing incentives for young people to continue to study beyond age 16; raising teaching and learning standards through a new Training Standards Council; establishing clear targets for skills and qualifications required nationally; building a qualifications system that is easily understood, gives equal value to both academic and vocational learning, meets employers' and individuals' needs, and promotes the highest standards; and working with business, employers and trade unions to support and develop skills in the workplace (see Chapter 5).

Each of these objectives is operationally defined and new instruments are set in motion for their implementation. Among these, and directly geared to the overall objective of widening adult participation in and access to learning, the most innovative are setting up a University for Industry and individual learning accounts.

A public–private partnership, the University for Industry (UfI) will be an open- and distance-learning organization which will have both individuals and businesses as customers. It will help people and businesses to identify the learning they need, and to access it through computers and broadcast media, at home or in the workplace, or by tapping into high-quality products and services through a network of learning centres to be set up around the country by organizations and local partnerships on a franchise basis. Initially, the university will focus on priority target areas covering basic skills, information and communication skills, the management of small- and medium-sized businesses and skills in specific industries and services. To get UfI started, the United Kingdom Government invested £15 million ($21.75 million) in 1998–99. It became operational in 2000.

A framework for a national system of individual learning accounts is also being set up. The two key principles behind this scheme are that individuals are best placed to choose what and how they want to learn, and responsibility for investing in learning is shared. Learning accounts will be available to everyone, including the self-employed. They will be used, at the learner's choice, to pay for learning – whether an evening class, or a learning programme bought through UfI, or meeting the cost of child care to allow time to study. In essence, they will be individual savings accounts with a bank or other financial institution, encouraged by government either through tax incentives or by matching the individual's contributions with public support. Local careers and guidance services will offer account holders information and advice about what and how to learn. As a first step £150 million ($217 million) will be made available to open a million accounts, each receiving £150 against a minimum of £25 from the account holder.

Additional support for these initiatives will be provided by the gradual development of the National Grid for Learning. It is designed to help teachers and students in schools access a wide range of learning materials on-line, including a virtual Teachers' Centre on the Internet. Finally, and as a clear indication of the seriousness with which these policy initiatives are being pursued, it is worth noting that a minister with special responsibility for lifelong learning has been appointed in the Department for Education and Employment.

Examples of other countries that have published national statements outlining their vision of lifelong learning can be briefly mentioned (OECD, 1998*a*).

In Finland's 1997 policy document, *The Joy of Learning: A National Strategy for Lifelong Learning*, the emphasis is on promoting broadly based continuous learning, combining 'learning careers' with activities in communities where people live and work. Policy objectives relate to personality development, strengthening democratic values and social cohesion, and meeting the challenge of internationalization, linked to an improved capacity for innovation, productivity and competitiveness. These objectives are shared by other Scandinavian countries, with their long-established tradition of adult and community-based education. In Norway's 1997 policy document, *The New Competence*, priority is placed on providing basic education for young people and adults who have missed out on initial education; on reinforcing co-operation between government and social partners to meet workplace learning needs; and on evaluating and recognizing learning wherever it takes place.

In the Netherlands, a year-long national Knowledge Debate resulted in 1997 in *Lifelong Learning: The Dutch Initiative*, an action programme to implement lifelong learning. It recognizes the broad meaning of lifelong learning, in which 'initial education forms a major link'. The rationale is both social and economic, and much of the programme revolves around the employability of workers and job applicants; the employability of teachers and researchers; and prevention of educational disadvantage through a reorientation of education starting from pre-school years. As in Norway, a social partnership model is strongly advocated. Underlining the specific lifelong learning needs of older workers, the long-term unemployed and women returning to the labour force, it stresses particular incentives for these groups. It also highlights the importance of collaboration between central, regional and local governments in strengthening the public infrastructure of vocational and adult education by developing strong and relatively independent regional educational centres.

Operational programmes arising from such policy frameworks are in their infancy and no conclusions can yet be drawn as to their efficacy. But although priorities between countries differ, it is possible to discern a number of convergent trends relating to the general concerns and directions of emerging policies for lifelong learning.

First of all, there is a clearly identified need to promote the widest possible participation in education and training of all age groups. Second, there is a realization that such expansion cannot be achieved by the public sector alone and there are calls, therefore, for partnerships and learning networks at central, regional and local levels. Third, for economic as well as social reasons (the two have to go together), priority is given to those who are most in need – the underprivileged and undereducated, unemployed adults and small businesses. And finally, great importance is attached both to meeting the needs of information and communication technologies and the effective use of these technologies in learning. These trends are also drawn out in specific target-oriented programmes.

Specific programme areas

The foundations of lifelong learning

Initial schooling
It is generally agreed that any strategy to implement lifelong learning must recognize the crucial role of initial basic schooling in providing a

sound foundation for all young people for subsequent learning and for life generally. But despite extensive school reforms in recent years, it is doubtful this has been driven by a lifelong-learning perspective. Moreover, a significant minority of young people – 15 to 20 per cent – continue to leave secondary schooling without having acquired any recognizable skills or qualifications for entry into working life or further study. In the context of lifelong-learning strategies, combating school failure remains a top priority.

Equally important is consensus among all concerned – educators, parents and employers – that what is expected of schools is not to produce specific job specialists but rather young people with a well-grounded all-round education, who have 'learned how to learn' and been endowed with interpersonal, communication and problem-solving skills, as well as the ability to use new information and communication technologies. These are non-curricular competences that call for a redefinition of the traditional core curriculum (for example, computing skills have become part of the new basics), for more active approaches to learning involving problem-solving pedagogies, and stronger links between subject-based theoretical knowledge and its practical applications. Traditional distinctions between academic and vocational learning fit poorly into this dynamic, lifelong-curriculum framework. The challenge is to develop flexible curricula opening up individualized learning paths, but which equip people with the essential competences and motivation to continue as lifelong learners (Istance, 1999).

It is in these directions that many OECD countries are now pursuing school-reform policies, in close co-operation with the organization under the 'Schools for Tomorrow' project of its Centre for Educational Research and Innovation (CERI).

Beyond compulsory schooling

Reform of upper secondary education has been, and continues to be, a central policy concern of most industrialized countries. This is the stage where the career patterns of young people are decided and where the effects of social-cum-educational disparities become most manifest. The debate revolves around the terminal versus the continuing education functions of this level of education, which are strongly associated with the vocational-academic divide, extending into tertiary education and nowhere yet satisfactorily bridged.

Because of youth unemployment and a growing social demand for education, the quasi-totality of young people of this age who now participate in various forms of education and training has sharpened the need to devise new, more individually based pathways to further learning and work. This is reinforced by a growing convergence between vocational and general education resulting from an increased component of theoretical knowledge in job-related preparation and recognition of the value of practical experience in academically related pursuits.

Existing pathways are of three types: (a) general academic education; (b) predominantly school-based vocational pathways leading to work, to further education or both (for example, in Sweden and, more recently, Greece); and (c) apprenticeship pathways in which learning within paid employment is combined with classroom learning (for instance the 'dual system' in German-speaking countries).

While the schooling model was favoured in earlier times, because it was judged more equitable, more recently apprenticeship systems of the German type have come into prominence because of their proven capacity to keep unemployment rates among 15- to 19-year-olds relatively low. Now, though, their popularity seems to be waning, partly because difficult economic times and increasing competition have made firms more reluctant to offer apprenticeships, and partly because more young people, in Austria and Germany as well, prefer to enrol in general rather than vocational and technical courses. From the individual's point of view, the main drawback of apprenticeships is that they do not leave open the possibility of entering tertiary education at a later date.

There is, thus, an emerging trend in a number of countries towards a broader approach to pathways that can meet the demand for conventional tertiary education and the requirements of the job market. Such double qualifying pathways include many types of early contact with the labour market, from formal apprenticeships to internships and student projects, and enabling students to see the world of work and study as intertwined, creating a positive attitude towards lifelong learning. There are studies which show that vocational approaches which qualify young people for both work and tertiary study are attractive, for example the Berufschochschulen (BHS) in Austria and Community Colleges in North America (OECD, 1998c).

In terms of the wider issue of how to develop coherent education, labour and social policies for young people preparing for work and lifelong learning, mention should be made of the youth guarantee approach that Nordic countries have been developing for the last two decades. This provides a guaranteed opportunity for all through a place in either education, training or work up to the age of 18 or 20 years. A system of incentives and penalties, with tight safety nets for those who fail, has helped make this approach work (Durand-Drouhin, 1998).

Tertiary education

Tertiary education, comprising universities and other institutions dispensing education beyond the upper secondary-school level, occupies an important role in the success of lifelong-learning strategies. It is a sector that, despite very significant expansion in participation in recent years, is set to continue to grow under the pressure of social demand. Tertiary qualifications have become the normal currency in many parts of high-skill labour markets and the demand for advanced learning goes well beyond that which is directly job related. It is also a sector that consumes large resources – mostly public – yet remains highly selective in terms of the social composition of its participants. Questions therefore arise about the organization, range and quality of learning available; about equity, particularly in relation to those who do not enter tertiary education; and about costs and financing.

These questions are at the heart of the debate on higher-education policies in many countries, and no doubt they will arise during the major European Union-conducted investigation into the role of higher-education institutions in lifelong learning. Three main issues can be identified for comment. Others, relating specifically to adult education, will be taken up later.

The first relates to the initial phase of higher education, in which half or more of the 20-year-olds in most OECD countries are now enrolled. Increasingly, the first years of higher education are seen as an extension of basic preparation for subsequent, more specialized studies – in other words, as part of the foundations for lifelong learning. Questions are thus raised about the nature and duration of initial tertiary education, and its ability to fulfil lifelong learning goals.

Second, tertiary institutions remain the chosen instruments for providing diverse possibilities for continuing education and training. Some opportunities are in the form of a return to conventional programmes, whether as 'second chance' entry or to augment previous experiences or diplomas. Many adults, however, are seeking flexible, individualized learning options at the tertiary level in their middle and later years that take forms other than conventional programmes. Despite the burgeoning demand for diversified adult learning, the institutional response remains relatively weak. Imaginative, bold initiatives will be required, with governments taking the lead in creating infrastructure, incentives and targets, and bringing into play the full potential of information and communication technologies as well as new partnerships among providers and between educational institutions, employers and community-based initiatives. In this respect the British experience – particularly the University for Industry and individual learning accounts – deserves close attention.

Finally, the diversification of programmes, clientèle and the functions of tertiary institutions in the lifelong-learning perspective requires a new approach to their recognition and certification systems and procedures. This is an area where institutions themselves should be encouraged to take the lead. While standards of achievement should not be diluted, the nature of achievement requires broadening beyond traditionally academic routes, to take account of learning outcomes acquired over time and in a variety of settings, including individualized learning and practical experience. The development of competence-based systems of qualifications and individual achievement profiles underway in a number of countries reflects a move in this direction. A modular approach to course construction in higher-education institutions would contribute to this objective.

Adult education

Adult education and training is the most crucial and problematic area for attaining lifelong learning. It is here where gaps between current and desirable levels of provision are greatest, and where inequalities are most marked. Political interest in this area has been heightened by the results of recent surveys of OECD countries which show that at least a quarter of adults fail to reach the minimum literacy levels needed to cope adequately with the demands of everyday life and work, let alone structural and economic change (OECD, 1995, 1997). The problems thus raised place education and training policies for this sector into the broader context of economic and social policies, particularly policies directed at combating social exclusion.

Difficulties in dealing with the adult education sector are compounded by its heterogeneous and segmented components. It comprises general adult education in formal settings, including vocational, basic skills and self-improvement or leisure education; labour market training for the unemployed and other special groups; and enterprise based training, both formal and informal. Responsibility for these different areas of activity is absent in some countries; in others it is spread between education and labour ministries at the central government level, regional and municipal authorities and, in some countries, employers and social-partner organizations.

Sources of funding are diverse. Employers provide most of the funds for enterprise-based training, with some government subsidy of training for apprentices and particular groups of employees, such as those facing redundancy or needing retraining as a result of restructuring. Training for the unemployed and difficult to employ is usually funded by the state, though employers make certain contributions in countries with compulsory training levy systems. General adult education may be funded by the state or by voluntary organizations, and often involves individual contributions through fees.

Such complexities make it difficult to generalize from country experience. It is clear that, because of the size and diversity of the groups concerned, all-inclusive policies are difficult to establish. The approach is therefore ad hoc, with different countries targeting specific groups and economic criteria predominating. Funding is the crucial factor, particularly when it comes to enterprise-based training. This is more prevalent in large companies than in medium and small ones, and in certain sectors. Those benefiting most tend to be those already better qualified and in senior positions. Women and part-time workers are less provided for than men and full-time workers. Under-investment in training and unequal distribution of training opportunities tend to reflect the unpredictability of training benefits. Measures to increase the transparency and portability of qualifications, as in the United Kingdom and the Netherlands, have helped make the benefits of training more predictable, thus encouraging personal investment. But although a variety of incentives are offered to firms and individuals, training remains underfunded and training markets underdeveloped.

To end on a more optimistic note, reference should be made to a case that comes closest to a comprehensive national policy on adult education: the Adult Education Initiative in Sweden. Aimed at halving unemployment by 2000, and at enabling disadvantaged groups to be brought closer to mainstream society, it is a good example of the Nordic tradition of seeking to achieve, through education, both economic growth and social equality.

Learning networks
The spread of educational networking represents one of the most visible manifestations of the lifelong-learning movement. Such networks operate both at national and international levels, not infrequently with links between the two. Essentially concerned with experimenting with new systems and ideas, their scope ranges from co-operative or joint projects to setting up organized arrangements for the exchange of experience and/or pooling of resources.

Under the SOCRATES and LEONARDO programmes of the European Commission, more than 100 projects have been devoted to increasing awareness of, and practice in, lifelong learning in and between European Union states. They include support for National Education Weeks, learning networks, learning journals and publications, curriculum-development activities, links with communities, and partnerships with business and other education organizations. The 1996 European Year of Lifelong Learning gave impetus to these activities by supporting, for example, transnational pilot projects focusing on training delivery in small and medium enterprises, and founding a large number of national organizations under the European Union Telematics Education and Training programme.

At national level, learning centres are coming into prominence in a number of countries. They are given a key role in the British White Paper – *The Learning Age* – which provides for close partnerships with regional, local and community authorities in defining their educational needs and co-ordinating measures to meet those needs. Developing local learning centres in communities, institutions and the workplace is a key aspect of the University for Industry.

In the Netherlands, under the 1996 Adult and Vocational Education Act, regional education centres (ROCs) have been set up under the responsibility of local authorities. They are formed through mergers of institutions involved in delivering secondary vocational education, apprenticeship and adult education, and have resulted both in a more flexible delivery service and in savings through more efficient use of accommodation and educational resources. In Italy, the Formazione Technico-professionale Superiore provides a highly integrated approach to lifelong learning through a consortium of secondary schools, universities, professional centres and enterprises in a particular region. In Japan, the Lifelong Learning Foundation in Kameoka was established in 1990 to promote all types of adult education with the support of local groups, corporations and enterprises.

In conclusion, and as a final example of networking, reference must be made to the OECD-sponsored project on Learning Cities (OECD, 1993). Its purpose has been to explore, through various examples, the degree to which cities can encourage a culture of lifelong learning. Initially, portraits of seven cities in seven OECD countries were developed. More recently five more have been added, illustrating the spread of interest in the idea of a 'learning city' in which lifelong learning occupies a central role in community development strategies. In the United Kingdom alone, more than twenty towns and cities are already active in this field, and will be drawn into the government's new lifelong-learning strategy.

Briefly, the idea of the learning city derives from the industrial shift occurring in many countries, leaving cities in a state of physical decline and with little social cohesion. Coupled with the now recognized centrality of learning and knowledge to modern economic activity and prosperity, one response is to shape urban regeneration projects in partnerships that include an important learning component, and to invest in formal and non-formal education and training, creating learning cities or regions. Developing such cities or regions will have the following characteristics: (a) a clear and sustained commitment from public authorities, education and research institutions, voluntary organizations and individuals to set learning at the heart of the city's development through partnerships; (b) a development strategy encompassing the whole range of learning, from early childhood to adult education; (c) creating globally competitive knowledge-intensive production and service activities, improving human and organizational capacities, and constructing environments conducive to learning, creativity and change; (d) a specific purpose and identity implying shared values and networks; and (e) social cohesion, environmental issues and cultural activities are an integrated part of the city's or region's development.

This provides the general framework, which the 'learning city' network endeavours to elucidate practically, based on the case studies of participating cities and regions.

Conclusions

This overview of national and international trends in lifelong learning points to a number of bottlenecks that have to be overcome if the rhetoric is to be converted, albeit gradually, into reality. Only a few of the more salient ones can be mentioned here.

First, developing a culture of lifelong learning has to be motivated by more than the economic rationale that dominates policy thinking at present, important though that undoubtedly is. Promotion and incentive policies directed at raising levels of participation in lifelong learning across all groups in society need to focus principally on influencing the attitudes of individuals, within a vision of society that is not only prosperous but also humane, just and culturally rich. Lifelong learning needs to become attractive to the individual and a high satisfaction in itself.

This cannot be achieved without radical change to the overall ethos of foundation education, involving transformation of the teaching/ learning process at school level and the eradication of school failure. Overcoming resistance to such changes, including that of parents and teachers, remains a major obstacle. Without progress in this area, those who are deprived of initial education will remain those who do not benefit from continuing education opportunities.

Second, in spite of persistent efforts to bridge the divide between general education and vocational education and training, the gap remains. This is a cultural phenomenon in societies that attach greater value to theoretical knowledge than to technical and vocational skills and competence. Redressing this imbalance should be a principal objective of those concerned with vocational education and training policies.

Third, it is clear that the level of employer involvement in lifelong-learning programmes is inadequate, even though many countries do not have information about the total contribution that enterprises make. Under-investment by firms is especially weak in the area of contribution to general vocational education and training, as distinct from what they pay for specific job-related training. The much vaunted desirability of partnerships will never become reality unless employers are persuaded to increase their contribution to lifelong learning, so they can gain collectively from the benefits that flow from a learning society.

This, finally, raises the question of the affordability of implementing policies for lifelong learning, particularly if the fight against social exclusion is taken seriously as a major objective of such policies. New resources are needed and these can only be marginally found by switching funds from other sectors of education or by applying efficiency and cost reducing measures in the delivery of learning opportunities. The use of information and communication technologies, essential to the spread of lifelong-learning systems, will itself involve significant extra resource outlays, at least initially. Public funding must be supplemented with increased contributions from individuals and employers if lifelong learning is to become a reality.

Under such circumstances, implementing lifelong learning policies can only be done incrementally and this is what is already happening in a number of countries. The challenge is to ensure that an incremental approach is planned and implemented within an agreed framework for the long-term realization of lifelong learning. The current debate on lifelong learning has at least opened up exciting new vistas for educational policy thinking.

References

Council of Europe. 1970. *Permanent Education*. Strasbourg, Council of Europe.

——. 1977. *Contents and Methods of Adult Education,* Strasbourg, Council of Europe.

——. 1978. *Permanent Education: Final Report*. Strasbourg, Council of Europe.

Cresson, E. 1996. Towards a Policy of Lifelong Learning. *Vocational Training* (Thessaloniki, Greece), No. 819, May–December, pp. 9–12.

Delors, J. 1996. Education: The Necessary Utopia (back cover of *Learning: The Treasure Within, Report to UNESCO of the International Commission on Education for the Twenty-first Century).* Paris, UNESCO Publishing.

Delors, J., et al. 1996. *Learning: The Treasure Within. Report to UNESCO of the International Commission on Education for the Twenty-first Century.* Paris, UNESCO Publishing.

D'Iribane, A. 1996. A Discussion of the Paradigms of the White Paper on Education and Training. *Vocational Training* (Thessaloniki, Greece), No. 819, May–December, pp. 23–31.

Durand-Drouhin, M. 1998. Opening Pathways from Education to Work. *OECD Observer*, No. 214, October/November.

European Union. 1993. *White Paper on Growth, Competitiveness and Employment*. Brussels, European Union.

——. 1995. *White Paper on Teaching and Learning: Towards the Learning Society*. Brussels, European Union.

——. 1997. *White Paper: Towards a Europe of Knowledge*. Brussels, European Union.

Faure, E., et al. 1972. *Learning to Be*. Paris, UNESCO.

Great Britain Department for Education and Employment. 1988. *The Learning Age: A Renaissance for a New Britain*, CM 3790. London: The Stationery Office.

Istance, D. 1999. Introduction: Schooling for Tomorrow and Lifelong Learning. *Innovating Schools*, Paris, OECD.

Kallen, D. 1996. Lifelong Learning in Retrospect. *Vocational Training* (Thessaloniki, Greece), No. 819, May–December, pp. 16–22.

Lengrand, P. 1970. *An Introduction to Lifelong Education*. Paris, UNESCO Publishing.

OECD. 1973. *Recurrent Education: A Strategy for Lifelong Learning*. Paris, OECD.

——. 1992. *High Quality Education and Training for All*. Paris, OECD.

——. 1993. *City Strategies for Lifelong Learning*. Paris, OECD.

——. 1995. *Literacy, Economy and Society*. Paris, OECD.

——. 1996. *Lifelong Learning for All*. Paris, OECD.

——. 1997. *Literacy Skills for the Knowledge Society*. Paris, OECD.

——. 1998a. *Education Policy Analysis*. Paris, OECD.

——. 1998b. *Human Capital Investment: An International Comparison*. Paris, OECD.

——. 1998c. *Pathways and Participation in Vocational and Technical Education and Training*. Paris, OECD.

Papadopoulos, G. 1994. *Education 1960–90: The OECD Perspective*. Paris, OECD.

2. The new frontiers of education[1]

Roberto Carneiro
Professor in the Study Centre on Peoples and Cultures
at the Catholic University of Portugal in Lisbon,
Editor in Chief of the *Journal of Education and Society,*
former Minister of Education in Portugal
and former President of TVI (Televisão Independente)

The future of education runs parallel to the circumstances of human-kind. After all, education has always been regarded as a kind of *pansofia* destined to make the most of knowledge and wisdom attained in the realm of each generation.

The unity of the person stretches across the influences of space and time. But behind this essential unity the human personality has developed a myriad of masks, as if seized by an inner drive to unfold in constant representations of the universe's major attribute: creativity.

As a consequence, every human development path has spawned cultural mutants. This intense cultural multiplication is displayed in a remarkable showcase of human diversity, for instance: *Homo faber* – tool cultures; *Homo socialis* – group-relations cultures; *Homo mediaticus* – communication cultures; *Homo ludens* – leisure cultures; *Homo economicus* – appropriation cultures; *Homo connectus* – net-working cultures; and *Homo sapiens* – interpretation cultures.

Indeed, we are now witnessing the emergence of a new breed of culture: that developed by *Homo connectus* or *collegatus* – a culture of on-line networking made possible by the immediacy of modern information and communication technologies. It is important to note that the initial stages of connectivity are directly linked to the needs of *Homo economicus*, increasing his mastery of the world.

1. This paper was written for UNESCO in September 1998.

The 'educating city'

The persisting prevalence of *Homo economicus* in our civilization creates serious imbalances in cities. Accumulation beyond human needs, and its legitimization by capitalistic modes of production, is eroding the social fabric and spreading exclusion to a level unforeseen in the theory of modern cities.

Rescuing our cities as symbols of human progress and places of memory thus appears a formidable and primordial task. A new city paradigm will have to respond to four major challenges, every one of them central to the rediscovery of the 'educating city', as Athens described itself in relation to Ancient Greece some 3,000 years ago. The four challenges to the post-industrial city are to foster urban intelligence, to stimulate urban learning, to build a common urban home and to reinvent urban democracy.

The concept of an educating city is propelled by a new social contract, a contract that seeks an urban redesign inspired by the notion of local neighbourhood. Restoring a human scale to the contemporary metropolis is a precondition for governance, the way to build up social capital and trust, the foundation for enhanced social cohesion and the strategy to arrive at 'high-touch' communities .

Only the effective consolidation of urban intelligence can overcome spiralling city opacity. Our urban conglomerates could then become subjects and engines of learning, loci of inclusiveness and participatory citizenship – referred to as building a common urban home and as the task of reinventing urban democracy.

The fates of cities and education are inextricably tied. It is not surprising that mounting tensions in the way we live together are reflected in new tensions in education. Indeed, education systems mirror with remarkable accuracy the contradictions of the societies they are devoted to serve. These tensions in education include: (a) the interplay between tradition and modernity; (b) the trade-offs involved in public policy-making; (c) strains between the long and the short term; (d) the search for increased equity in a world dominated by fierce competition; (e) the need to reconcile global (universal) approaches with local (individual) needs; (f) an ever-growing expansion of knowledge with limited human capacity to assimilate it; and (g) the delicate interplay between the spiritual and the material.

Societal outlooks

In the light of this broad perspective it is possible to spell out three major societal trends that provide the context for education development in the twenty-first century. These issues were broadly identified in *Learning: The Treasure Within* – the report presented to UNESCO in April 1996 by the International Commission on Education for the Twenty-first Century, chaired by Jacques Delors.[2] They are the interplay between globalization and the search for roots; the quest for social cohesion, inclusion and increased democracy; and the transition from inequitable economic growth to sustainable human development.

The three phenomena address in a global setting the main social, cultural and economic challenges faced by humankind at the turn of the century. Investigating them from an educational angle involves far-reaching changes to the way educational priorities are cast. And, inevitably, this somewhat controversial choice of the major challenges facing societies at the dawn of a new millennium calls for some kind of educational response.

This analysis inspired the Delors Commission to put forward its vision for education in the twenty-first century. The vision rests on four priorities, or 'pillars': learning to be, learning to know, learning to do, learning to live together.

The specific recommendations regarding each pillar are extensively developed in *Learning: The Treasure Within*. But it is interesting to understand how these broad categories of learning priorities relate to the so-called strategies of knowledge-based societies so widely heralded as the new mainstream paradigm.

The World Bank's 1998 edition of the *World Development Report* symptomatically elects this theme as a priority. 'Knowledge for Development' is now the name of the game, well attuned to the growing demands of the 'cognocratic' society. Likewise, new growth theories that are very much inspired by the contribution of human knowledge to the creation and diffusion of technological innovations indicate four pillars of modern sustainable development: skilled people, knowledge institutions, knowledge networks and information infrastructures.

These dramatic changes towards the valuing of intangible

2. Roberto Carneiro was a member of the International Commission on Education for the Twenty-first Century.

economies and immaterial societies have once again propelled education to the centre stage of strategic thinking. In addition, learning is developing into a kind of post-modern ideology. Curiously, in an era of diffuse ideologies, human intelligentsia seem to have found something new to cling to. Learning individuals, learning communities, learning organizations and learning nations represent a consensual agenda for the future.

In this comprehensive approach exists what could constitute a sound basis for a new social contract. We speak of a broad partnership intertwining both rights and obligations that are significant to knowledge-based societies' concerns. In this perspective, education is not simply the exercise of a universally recognized right. It is also the reverse – the exercise of learning as a moral duty, an integral part of citizenship and of the obligation to be socially active in a rapidly evolving environment.

New knowledge

Now that we have arrived at knowledge as a core concept of our societies, it is possible to contend that educational institutions are not simply faced with a quantitative challenge. It is an undisputed fact that knowledge is expanding at an unprecedented rate. The most puzzling mutation, however, is that which affects the ultimate nature of knowledge.

New knowledge is undergoing constant metamorphosis. The most important change concerns the transition from objective knowledge (codified and scientifically organized) to subjective knowledge (a personal construct, intensely social in its processes of production, dissemination and application).

In the case of personal-cultural knowledge, following a new typology of knowledge patterns for post-industrial societies, social intercourse is a primeval agent. Memory, cultural background, family contexts, ethnic heritages, language of emotions – all these factors have strong bearing on the paths to building and acquiring knowledge.

Education and training strategies will need to adapt to the new knowledge patterns contained in the immense variety of human mindsets, accepting that knowledge is very much a personal construct implicitly recognizing a variety of roads leading to its timely appropriation. The major impacts on education and training in knowledge-based societies are moves from objective to constructive knowledge, an industrial to a learning society, instruction to personal learning, communication to knowledge acquisition and schooling to non-formal modes of learning.

New ways of knowing

Knowing is not a simple operation, or an immediate yield of teaching. We are tempted to make very complex the conceptual ways of knowing by differentiating between at least four distinct ways (Figure 1):

Fig. 1. Four ways of knowing

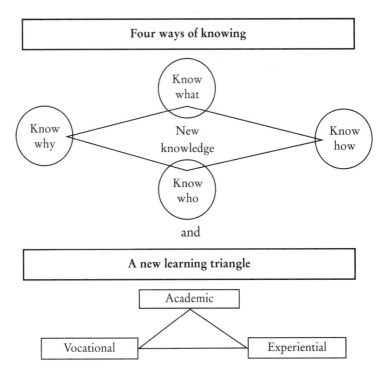

Knowing 'what' and 'why' corresponds to traditional visions surrounding teaching: objective knowledge constructed and rotely transmitted around the notions of causal effects. Knowing 'who' and 'how' pays justice to the softer aspects of knowledge production, which appear to be highly contingent on social and cultural environments.

A new learning triangle links academic, vocational and experiential learning. With this approach in mind, experience – learning by doing – is a powerful way to enhance learning, particularly in all that concerns *metis* (practical knowledge) as opposed to *episteme* (theoretical knowledge) or *techne* using the old Greek classification. Learning thus requires increasing flexibility. It tends to take place everywhere, unlike traditional modes of teaching, which can only occur in highly formalized settings.

Since the World Conference on Education for All (Jomtien, Thailand, 1990) there has been a conceptual shift in thinking about learning, away from traditional school as the dominant mode of delivery towards multiple modes in which learning can occur in the same place or different places, at the same time or at different times. This leads to four kinds of learning modes: the traditional school – same time and same place; shift or year-round education – different times, same place; open university – same time, different places; and flexible learning – different times and different places.

The transition from traditional school to flexible learning represents the conceptual switch from Jomtien and its appealing call for a worldwide 'education for all' movement to a 'learning throughout life for all' approach, which is more in line with the new requirements of the knowledge-based society.

To make the most of this philosophy of education, 'learning to know' will also have to drift away from Western-biased axioms of cognition: away from a strictly Western canon of knowledge to a more global one open to the best epistemic contributions of all cultures and human stories.

The simple rational algorithms of a purely Eurocentric canon fall short of the explanations needed to interpret a complex, uncertain world. Only a polysemic approach to knowledge can provide the means of overcoming fragmentation and linearity. Further, effective progress and social development strongly depend on generators of diversity rather than systems of standardization.

The modern reality is filled with complexity. Complexity tends to evolve into self-organizing systems based on emergent properties. My fundamental submission is that 'learning' becomes the emergent property of biological organizations. These entities are capable of reaching higher forms of self-organization, unlike their purely mechanical peers.

Fig. 2. Knowing to know

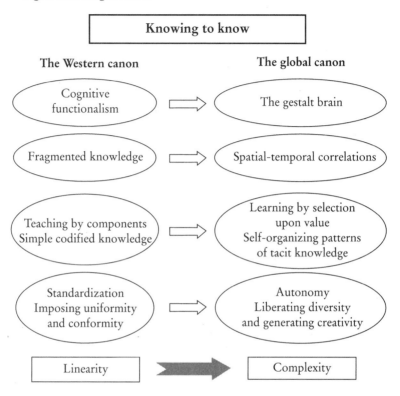

Inclusive knowledge is the step forward, knowledge that escapes the classical teaching approach to revolve around flexible learning processes aimed at cognitive achievements, metacognitive skills (the ability to self-regulate learning efforts) and acquiring 'soft' or social skills.

Future learning contents will then address a wealth of human needs, not merely the production of professional skills or economic assets, as was the norm in industrial society and prescribed by its human capital derivatives. Following this approach, we can classify the human advancement needs for learning throughout life into three main categories: (a) personal and cultural development; (b) social and community development, and (c) professional development and sustainable employability.

The first pertains to the sphere of inner coherence and to the related necessity of meaning-making throughout life: this is the territory where

Homo sapiens builds sense. The second category contemplates the wealth of citizenship requirements in an active democracy as well as participatory skills in a fully social entrepreneurship: the formation of social capital and the thrust towards enhanced social cohesion. The third category addresses the productive person and his or her challenge of sustainable employability throughout the entire life-span.

This comprehensive understanding of educational needs is what society is demanding as what could be called 'higher-level basic skills'. These basic skills largely transcend the classical debates concerning the core curriculum and its learning outcomes.

Seen in this broader framework, learning throughout life is a multidimensional effort. In the light of what we earlier proposed, it becomes a central motto, a sort of compulsive ideology, to shape our unfolding societies. To summarize, we can now speak of six prime directions for learning throughout life: diversity of itineraries, continuing learning opportunities, community participation, antidotes to unlearning and deskilling, social dimensions to knowledge production and remedies to the inequitable distribution of intelligence.

These directions will set the scenario and the pace for profound reform of our education systems. The outcome is difficult to envisage at a distance, but one thing is sure: the old paradigms of a rote industrial mode of production, reflected in hierarchical school organization, will require profound re-engineering.

Learning throughout life is no longer a simple extension of a two-stage imagery: the mere sequence of initial-cum-further education. The concept calls for a wide reconsideration of a lifetime allocation to learning, embracing the emerging phenomena of the new elder, the flexible organization of work and combined strategies of productive learning activities.

Practical propositions

Finally, it is possible to develop some practical proposals inspired by the basic propositions to the international community advanced in the Delors report. To try to foresee some public policies that could have practical impact on institutional change, I shall put forward three strategic ideas: study-time entitlement after compulsory schooling, teachers at the centre of learning opportunities, and the dual system of overcoming the 'trust gap' between companies and schools.

The first would be to stimulate a demand-driven lifelong-learning system through study-time entitlements offered after compulsory schooling.

The second idea involves placing teachers at the centre of learning opportunities. Indeed, there is a worrying trend in public policies to disinvest from teachers. Conversely, a strong plea should be made to invest in the teaching force to make it the major source of content provision in an information-led world. Offering teachers appropriate authoring tools, hardware and software, accompanied by intensive retraining opportunities, would motivate many to overcome the passive model of the past: being told how to perform and condemned to use prescribed materials developed by someone else.

Third, I strongly favour a dual system of learning, designed to bridge codified and tacit knowledge and equipped to overcome the traditional opposition between humanities and professional studies. It is time that our civilization surpassed old thinking that relinquishes general culture to vocational skills. If other arguments were absent, it would suffice to listen to the growing claims of employers that imparting basic and social skills is more important than training for narrow professional aptitudes.

Education and learning are key priorities in determining the design of a twenty-first century that will be better than the previous one. International co-operation in this field thus requires further impetus and stronger commitment.

Three major steps are required in any effort to inspire break-through momentum in the international community. A knowledge-based society can only seek moral justification on grounds of greater equity than its predecessor model. These steps are debt swaps for education, exchange of scientists and researchers, and earmarking a quarter of development aid for education.

The twenty-first century brings fresh hope. Learning is truly the treasure contained within these new times. The industrial society's legacy is a generation of consumers and producers, which does not reflect well on humanity. The learning society opens the road to a generation of creators.

3. Lifelong learning: old achievements, future challenges

Maria Teresa Ambrósio
Professor at the Universidade
Nova de Lisboa
and President of the National
Council of Education, Lisbon

To learn throughout life is neither an abstract concept nor a new proposal. Rather, it is an approach to life, pursued with effort but which brings great satisfaction and pleasure.

My own experience of lifelong learning taught me that: the great deal I learned at the start of my career as an educational planner from work done by the OECD, which became the basis for further thought for many of my generation. Later, UNESCO programmes gave me access to new guidelines and interrogation, to new roles in education and development processes in different countries. Contacts with the World Bank, particularly its support programmes for Portuguese-speaking African countries, provided a wealth of material for further thought on educational policies and finally led me to political and academic life. Lifelong learning can be a working, satisfactory experience when it is well thought out and adopted with conviction. As we enter the new millennium, it is time to take stock of what has already been done, and what is yet to be done, to promote the major challenge of lifelong learning.

What is lifelong learning?

The challenge of lifelong learning involves adding meaning to new strategic approaches to educational policy for the twenty-first century. After all, lifelong learning is no more than an approach – a wider reaching route to be taken by children, adolescents, adults and senior citizens in all the different locations and situations involved in education and training throughout life. To be more precise:

> it is the process of an aware, personal construction of the individual, through learning and education but also through existential experience to which thought has been given, conditioned by multiple, interpersonal, social relationships. Simple learning, or the teaching–learning relationship, is no more than the cognitive dimension on which the acquisition of explicit, practical, tacit learning is based, essential pillars for the development of thought, reasoning, logic, analysis, synthesis and questioning – all the cognitive skills that help the individual to know how to learn, with the support of whoever is assisting, or alone.

Learning how to learn is also a specific challenge in today's information society. It is learning how to seek information, analyse it, use it and change it daily into knowledge. This cognitive dimension should not be separated from other dimensions, such as developing friendly and social relationships, or from the ethical and aesthetic experience of each individual, or from social responsibility, in fact from all that current theoretical trends in education refer to as the holistic and self-styled process of lifelong training. Education and training in the information society is the starting point, however, and that means we must rethink the education we have and reinvent new processes, new systems and new educational policies.

The need for change

Current formal school systems, informal activities taking place around schools and vocational training systems that are more or less official, more or less geared to the job market (or to labour markets or economies), or even aimed at inserting those who tend to be marginalized into social life, do not stand up to an evaluation of the demands made by lifelong learning.

We have to rethink and analyse in the light of the goals of lifelong learning all of the issues that today figure among the concerns of politicians: (a) reorganization of curricula throughout the school system (particularly towards the end of secondary education) and of school strategies, training plans and vocational training; (b) the impact of using multimedia provided by the information society; (c) frameworks of reference for assessing pupils; (d) traditional examinations and tests; (e) models for teacher training and its assessment; and (f) evaluating schools from early childhood development to university level.

We are experiencing a period of change, especially in education culture, and with it all the references used to organize our education systems. What was valid in past decades is no longer entirely valid today, particularly in terms of what we want for the future. We are not afraid to rethink issues for the present, because we have sufficiently solid experience to learn continually to revise education policy.

The future is constant guided change, and not only structural reforms or improvements to existing quality. Rather, it is change that entails inevitable breaks with the past, so that we can make qualitative progress that will force us to think less about organized, well-administered systems and more about how to conduct dynamic learning and training processes, which are present both within and outside the systems we already have.

My view is that, essentially, educational policy is the specific, possible reflection of social feeling: there can be no quality of life or human development without education and without ongoing learning.

The major goals in training citizens as human resources – for a development that requires knowledge, a solidly based scientific culture and adequate technological skills to be able to act effectively – will all have to be the result of multiple programmes and activities within school systems, assisted by training centres and colleges.

But another objective is educating people for active citizenship, so they can be aware and intelligently understand the world around them, have a committed social response, and build together ethical values that will enable us to live in peace.

These are the major objectives of overall educational activity, and are not a mission that can be reduced to the state. It is a responsibility that appeals to states, but generally they wish to create another model able to guide this whole educational approach. One that is multisectoral, multiregulating, multiparticipative, multiterritorial for the educational society. It is a model that demands revising the socio-educational contract (particularly in Europe) on which our education systems are based, our basic laws and criteria for evaluation, all of which have been built up patiently over the century just past and the decades in which most of us have been working.

This is an indispensable background that allows us to work at the pace of education and not at the pace of the social change we are now witnessing, remembering that the pace of education is long, slow and existential. It allows us to rethink and reinvent a new educational paradigm in the light of which we can evaluate what we have done, what we are doing and what we want to achieve.

As always, international co-operation has a fundamental role to play. It will help above all with reflection and the dissemination of reflection. It will lead to new management policies and the convergence of strategies, and will sustain solidarity. But it will always be for educators in each country – parents, teachers, instructors and social promoters – to conduct well-thought-out change in our education structures, in our aspirations and the opportunities and problems we face, trying to find the right approach and political view for the changes we desire. Promoting lifelong learning today means reflecting, inquiring, experimenting, observing, witnessing, assessing results and once again reflecting on what we have done.

Teaching from a new perspective

Lifelong learning, of course, is not just about macro-decisions. We also need to consider those who are learning and those who are teaching. We need to become aware of very specific problems that have to be confronted at the chalk face. There are several issues that need to be further debated, which arise from querying teaching models from the point of view of lifelong learning.

The individual process of lifelong learning

It is important clearly to explain basic concepts when talking about lifelong learning. One is found in certain research into adult learning, conceived as a process for developing the individual. It is a process involving the permanent acquisition of new knowledge, whether it is tacit daily knowledge or practical, vocational, explicit knowledge – the kind of learning that can be organized into epistemological disciplines.

But constructing the individual is also a process that, particularly in adults, develops constantly with the acquisition of skills, attitudes and professional and social behavioural patterns based on individual reflection and on living experiences. Adult learning is very different from child and adolescent learning. To be effective, it must always be founded on reference to the sociocultural and economic pillars of which adults are part, and particularly to their own experiences of life.

In this approach, adult learning is not merely rational but is also a process that is clearly identified with the individual, who builds his or her social and personal identity through relationships – sometimes conflictual, sometimes through dialogue – with the professional, social and family environments, and the surrounding human environment.

Lifelong learning is not just a question of policy for school education. Rather, it is based on the need for individuals to respond to the social dynamics of change. To a certain extent this change can be explained by economic or social change or competition. But it can also be explained, in certain areas and in some less privileged groups, by the dynamics of community living, by a crisis, a development strategy or even survival.

The emergence of learning in society

This change in concept from school learning (defined by educational policy) to an ongoing process of education and training which is the individual's response to society, is extremely important and must be remembered in discussions and in analysing paradigms for those who teach and for how they teach.

Clearly this changed concept arises with the emergence of a new type of 'pupil', an apprentice or 'social individual who learns'. This new type of learner is not just an individual pupil who learns, but is immersed in a dynamic society that trains him or her. Lifelong learning is a process rooted not only in a movement towards a more autonomous individual, but also in the new relationships that this individual establishes throughout life with many and varying social institutions that do not allow the person to become isolated from the world or from the surrounding environment.

The phenomenon of ongoing learning, and learning from experience, queries traditional educational theories and gives rise to a new type of 'andragogic' paradigm, alongside positivist-pedagogic school paradigms, based not on an objective view of building the individual but on an anthropo-formative view developed according to the dynamics of training–action–training.

This is lifelong learning, but it is a new way of learning. As some authors claim: 'Life is only life if it involves learning' (Mezirow, 1996). Learning is not just cognitive reasoning, it means developing the personal system, and we know very well that the psychology of adult development has had a great deal to say on this subject (Knowles, 1990).

Changing pedagogic paradigms

So what is teaching? Is it teaching from the new perspective of lifelong learning? We are aware of school models and of elaborate vocational training models and the innovations they have brought to teaching/learning. These are universal models rooted in Piaget's psychology, and in concepts of cognitive constructivism used in the school environment (*in vitro*), which in recent decades have developed from more central perspectives – from teacher, school, class or pupil perspectives.

In brief, these models can be represented as the three-sided relationship expressed in pedagogic triangle diagrams, which teachers know well. The school triangle (Figure 1) explains learning as a three-sided relationship between the teacher, learning and the pupil: the teacher teaches, but knows that teaching does not automatically mean that the pupil learns. The teacher must establish with the pupil an educational relationship – a personal relationship – to mobilize cognitive capacities and motivation. Only this will stimulate in the pupil the capacity to learn.

Fig. 1. School pedagogic triangle

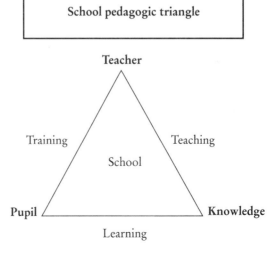

However, pedagogic paradigms more geared to adults or to vocational training (Figure 2) represent a more complete process. The teacher or trainer is the person able to establish a two-sided relationship between learning, the individual and the professional activity, developing a didactic logic between the individual and knowledge. The teacher may not teach but has to get across to the pupil the need to seek knowledge and information. The teacher must impart to the individual a social, professional and personal comprehension of what the profession is, and try to develop between the individual and the profession continuous dynamics for personal and professional development. Vocational training is no longer school learning geared to school age adolescence.

Fig. 2. Formative strategy triangle (Mezirow, 1996; Honoré, 1992; Pineau, 1995; Knowles, 1990)

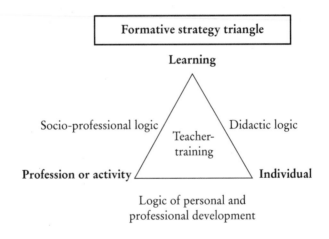

There is also the 'alternating teaching-learning model', widely known nowadays from initial school training up to university level, in which the aim is to include in the learning process what we call theoretical knowledge, practical knowledge and vocational experience.

Unfortunately, alternating models have lower status because they usually refer to vocational training – to the acquisition of 'know how' which is still highly stigmatized by the hierarchy – academically supported between 'practical knowledge' and 'production' and 'spiritual learning'. Alternating models are above all pedagogic paradigms closely linked to short-term vocational training. But from our experience, they give good results even in some advanced training courses.

Research efforts into processes of adult learning have made a considerable contribution towards analysis of current practices. They have allowed us to approach adult training with explanatory models for cognitive development for all adults, whether they be adolescents, workers or intellectuals. Research trends in this field, whether English- or French-speaking in origin, are the same on this basic point: that the development of autonomous individuals is not achieved alone by the homoeostatic adaptation used in *in vitro* learning but by morpho-genetic transformations in difficult, vital situations of survival, conflict, competition and progress. It is what, in contrast with the school context, some authors call *in vivo* learning (Pineau, 1995).

It is for this reason that learning models and adult training are not based, and should not be based, on the systematic, intentional, sequential, disciplinary nature of the direct relationship between theory and practice. Rather, they are guided by the development of cognitive processes based on performance capacity, on the capacity to seek information, and on the capacity to change learning and knowledge into projects for action or further investigation. It is the search for a meaning, for a personal meaning in educating adults.

Can we live with this dual approach, with these two teaching para-digms, and allow them to continue in school and post-school years, or will there have to be a break between them in future?

At the moment, all we can say is that the different models co-exist in educational and vocational training systems – learning for children and adolescents, and post-school models for adult learning. In the field of adult education there is a wealth of experience. Particularly when there is a context and location for this experience, it can be used to resolve problems in special groups or communities, or even for specific projects: for instance, adult education for community development, refreshing the knowledge of managers or vocational training for special groups, such as women in long-term employment. Such experiences are excellent for adult education's diversity and setting.

What we do not know is whether the co-existence of the school-teaching and post-school models eases development of the ongoing process of lifelong learning. Between the school model and the adult model there is a period during which, some researchers claim, there is 'delearning'. We are aware, for example, of problems around adolescents and professions. These are not just problems of knowledge being ill adapted. We also know from studies that there are difficulties in re-adapting and mobilizing knowledge. We must therefore ask whether the traditional pedagogic school model should continue, or whether within the school system we should develop other models more appropriate to the maturity of individuals, bearing in mind the potential provided by the information society and the creation of multiple education centres where hetero-, self- and eco-training can be given.

A conclusion, however, can be drawn from an analysis of current teaching models and practices: school teaching models do not contain the dynamics and initiative required for continued learning in adulthood. To assume sense in, and to invest in, lifelong learning is a fundamental learning process for adults. I do not believe that only economic benefits or improvement in social status are the main motives for adult learning, or that they are the only forces that lead to maintaining lifelong learning or continuing to benefit from it.

What to teach and who does the teaching?

In querying pedagogic models we must still ask: What do we teach, and who does the teaching? These questions are pertinent to school-education policies but are particularly relevant to lifelong learning. For learning, which was initially designed as the sum of the steps in acquiring knowledge and the development of cognitive capacities, is today an ongoing, autonomous process throughout the life of the individual.

This leads to querying the existing school programmes and teachers. Similarly, the results expected at the end of school – which we usually assess through examinations and reward with diplomas – will have to be revised, depending no longer on the end of the learning process but on its continuity. These are questions also raised in school teaching. In new perspectives on school teaching it is no longer the content that is queried, but the epistemological value and the cognitive potential of acquired knowledge: curricular assessment should not be done so much from the perspective of fundamental, practical or operative knowledge, understanding or cognitive logic, but on knowledge and skills that will lead to lifelong learning.

What should we learn? Learn to handle knowledge, learn intelligent reference to the real world, learn to face problems, learn to analyse systematically, and learn to develop complex and multidisciplinary thought. Learning through planning, learning from problems, learning by querying experience and by observation, are all new emancipatory paradigms reflecting the educational activity of teaching/learning that must be present when we think of new learning strategies.

The final question to be asked is: Who does the teaching? Who are the new teachers? There are teachers in school systems, but there are instructors in vocational training systems as well as tutors, leaders and fellow travellers in the learning process who are gaining status in different teaching/learning experiences. We do not know what future teachers will be like. We do know that teaching/educating/training is a multifaceted task in the formative human relationship, which demands knowledge, of course, but also a considerable capacity for empathy, communication and even greater intellectual acumen.

This is not a technical profession for conducting predefined functions, but rather a social mission, a recognized social activity demanding ongoing learning at a high level. Only the future will tell if it finds new locations for work, and a new status in a society for education.

It is a good idea to remember some programmes currently underway, which seem far removed from lifelong training problems. They are the 'strategic training plans', which in major institutions and companies – so-called 'qualifying' institutions or companies – have had very interesting results. Basically they are collective training models, community training geared to a specific strategy in which everyone understands the meaning of the training. Using considerable resources and interpersonal support, they provide interesting ground for analysis. It is worth looking at them in detail because, although they are linked to the world of economy, production and human resources management, they are closer than we sometimes suspect to problems with lifelong learning.

Lastly, it must be emphasized that in the demand for human dignity and defence, no action plan for lifelong learning, no matter how urgent it is, can overlook the indispensable nature of research and ongoing, critical reflective evaluation, the supreme reference always being the individual viewed globally and the subject of all learning. Dialogue between the research community, specialists, politicians and system administrators is more essential than ever before. The preparatory framework for educational policies that we used from the 1960s to the 1990s is no longer adequate for understanding the social activity that is education and lifelong learning.

References

Fabre, M. 1994. *Penser la formation*. Paris, PUF.

Galvani, P. 1991. Autoformation et Fonction de Formateur. *La Chronique Sociale* (Lyon).

Honoré, B. 1992. Vers l'Œuvre de Formation. *L'ouverture à l'existence*, Paris, L'Harmattan.

Knowles, M. 1990. *L'apprenant adulte: vers un nouvel art de la formation*. Paris, Les Éditions de l'Organisation.

Meirieu, P. 1994. *Apprendre . . . Oui, mais comment?* Paris, ESF (1st ed., 1987).

Mezirow, J. 1996. Contemporary Paradigms of Learning. *Adult Education Quarterly*, Vol. 46, No. 3, pp. 158–73.

Pineau, G. 1995. Recherches sur l'autoformation existentielle: des boucles étranges entre auto et exoréférences. *Éducation Permanente* (Paris), No. 122.

4. Developing-country challenges

Toby Linden
Knowledge Co-ordinator,
Secondary Education,
Human Development Network,
the World Bank

The World Bank is quite new to issues of learning throughout life and still has a lot to find out. But lifelong learning is relevant to the work the Bank does – and profoundly relevant to the developing countries with whom the Bank primarily deals.

Over the past three decades the developing world has made a great deal of progress on education. For example, while thirty years ago less than half of children of primary-school age were attending school, the proportion is now more than three-quarters. In the same period, the percentage of children attending secondary school doubled from a little over 20 to 45 per cent, and the participation rate in tertiary education trebled from around 4 to 14 per cent of young people of tertiary-level age.

A different sort of achievement, but an important one none the less, has been increased attention focused on education and training by all governments and agencies concerned with development issues. Progress made with respect to primary education, for instance, would not have been possible without the World Conference on Education for All held in Jomtien, Thailand, in 1990.

Some education problems

These are genuine achievements. But developing countries face specific and significant problems, which fall into four categories.

First, in the past few years there has been faltering in progress made on access to education. In sub-Saharan Africa, enrolment rates are now declining. There, as well as in South Asia, Latin America and the Caribbean, within five years of starting primary education, more than a third of pupils drop out. So while governments have persuaded parents to send their children to school and have invested resources in offering basic education to all, after a short period a significant proportion are deciding that education is not worth while.

Second is the issue of unequal access to education. In the developing world, improved enrolment figures mask considerably lower participation rates for women, minorities, the poor and people in rural areas.

Quality is a third major issue. Even in high-income countries with well-established education systems, there are high levels of illiteracy among populations. We do not have comprehensive figures for the developing world, but we do know it faces the same problem. Good-quality education is crucial: poor quality squanders resources, and can drive people out of education and training systems, thus wasting the efforts governments and others invest in them. As a result, people, communities and countries are not receiving the knowledge and skills needed to achieve high levels of development.

A fourth big problem is weak institutional capacity. Governments and institutions in many developing countries are not equipped to deal with current education problems – and now they face the additional challenge of substantially reforming their education systems.

Implications for learning throughout life

All these problems, of course, place developing countries at a great disadvantage in attempting to move towards to a learning society. Growing populations in the developing world will place even more pressure on stressed education and training systems. Without access to education, individuals cannot even travel on the road to learning – let alone the road to lifelong learning.

If a learning society is about anything, it is about everybody having access to education – and equitable access to learning throughout life. This is a moral and an economic imperative. Countries with poor records as regards easy and fair access to education, especially where this is the result of structural disadvantages or cultural norms, are on the wrong side of history.

Regarding the quality of education, developing countries face a double threat with respect to lifelong learning. Poor-quality teaching already condemns too many young people to low levels of achievement. But the learning society shifts the goal-posts further: students not only need high levels of achievement, they also need new skills and new attitudes to become lifelong learners.

The weak institutional capacity of developing countries is a major obstacle on the path towards lifelong learning. Creating a learning society requires profound shifts in the roles of actors in an education and training system, in society as a whole and, most profoundly, in the role of government. The poor management and institutional capacity of governments and institutions in developing countries place them at a particular disadvantage. How are they to implement the shifts needed to create a learning society? Indeed, how are they even to grasp the nature of these shifts and begin to set priorities for implementation?

The relevance of lifelong learning

Under such circumstances, it is tempting to suggest that notions of learning throughout life have little relevance for developing countries. There are two main arguments made in this respect.

The first is that their education systems are not sufficiently developed. Two random instances illustrate this difficulty. In Burkina Faso almost four in five adults are illiterate, the enrolment ratio in primary school is less than 40 per cent and it drops to less than 10 per cent in secondary education. On another continent, Guatemala has adult literacy rates of 67 per cent and strong primary-education enrolment of 88 per cent, but participation in secondary education drops to 26 per cent.[1] Both examples say something about students' perceptions of the value of secondary education, and place a question mark over the feasibility of encouraging learning throughout life.

A second argument against the relevance of lifelong learning to developing countries is that their economies do not demand high levels of knowledge, and do not require the new and flexible skills on which learning throughout life is based. The argument continues along the lines that the comparative advantage of lesser developed economies is the availability of cheap labour. Labour is generally cheap because the

1. Data concerning literacy and enrolment are taken from the World Education Indicators in the *World Education Report 2000*. Paris, UNESCO Publishing, 2000.

people involved are unskilled. Indeed, what need does a gardener, for instance, have to learn throughout life?

This argument is plainly wrong. Lifelong learning has nothing to do with the stages of development of a country – all countries need to think about learning throughout life, for the following reasons.

First, with regard to unskilled labour, of course all societies have some need for manual labour. But we know that the number of jobs involving manual work is decreasing and that labour is made more efficient through the application of knowledge – in the gardener's case, knowledge of fertilizers, growing conditions, genetic structures, etc.

Second, the economic crisis of the late 1990s in East Asian and other countries shows the impact of external shocks on the global and national economies, and how dramatically an economic situation can change. Response to such shocks and the ability to avoid them depends on the adaptability and flexibility of a work force.

Third, some developing countries are already fully conscious of the lifelong-learning agenda. Argentina, Chile, Hungary and the transitional economies of Central Europe generally are just a few. A look at their figures reveals a quite different picture from that of countries already mentioned. Argentina, for instance, has an adult illiteracy rate of 3.4 per cent, which matches or betters some OECD countries. Enrolments in secondary education are 77 per cent and in tertiary education over 36 per cent. On another continent, Hungary has an illiteracy rate of less than 1 per cent, almost 100 per cent enrolment in secondary education and gross enrolment ratio of 24 per cent in tertiary education. These are substantial achievements of mature education systems. Although such countries receive support and in some cases loans from the World Bank, they are clearly in a different category.

There is a fourth reason why it is wrong to think about 'stages of development' in the context of lifelong learning. There is strong evidence in OECD countries that the undereducated face declining prospects. At a conference on prospects for youth, sponsored by the OECD and the United States Department of Education (Washington D.C., February 1999), it was striking that the OECD and many developing countries share the problem of a growing core of disaffected youth who are spending longer and longer outside the mainstream of society. There may be differences of scale between countries, but in both developed and developing nations there is a keen policy focus on this issue and a belief that lifelong learning is part of the answer.

Meeting challenges through lifelong learning

There is another argument against the relevance of lifelong learning to developing countries which deserves more careful attention. Crudely, it goes something like this: developing countries have plenty to worry about – among other things the four education problems identified at the start of this chapter – without having to be concerned about learning throughout life. There is truth in this, in the sense that any successful move towards a learning society needs improved institutional capacity to ensure equitable access to education for all and quality learning environments.

The World Bank has been working with developing countries for thirty-five years to help improve their education systems and tackle the major problems they have. Its lending programme has grown over the years, and currently stands at around $2 billion a year. And the Bank recently produced a new education strategy that will take forward its learning programme.

The question is whether thinking about a learning society will help developing countries meet their education challenges. Only if there is a positive answer to that question can we really say that lifelong learning is relevant to them. My feeling is that it is, for the following reasons:

The need for change

A learning society demands new roles for actors in education systems. It demands new types of financing and other mechanisms in new demand-led systems, and it requires certification on the basis of competences rather on time served in institutions. Given that developing countries have to reform their education systems to meet the challenges already identified, it makes sense for them to undertake reform within a policy framework of lifelong learning. If developing countries created primary education systems that were pupil-led and imparted skills that enabled individuals to acquire knowledge both now and in the future, there would be measurable improvements in quality – and they would be on the road to lifelong learning.

Secondary education reform

Secondary education is at the heart of a learning society. Unless secondary education is made a powerful and effective phase of an individual's educational life, lifelong learning will never be a reality. This is a key issue for developing countries as they face increasing primary enrolments and strong social pressures to expand secondary education. Many countries have high enrolments in secondary education but quality remains a major challenge, and in almost every country in the developing world there are rigid secondary education and training systems. Such issues need to be addressed and all require change. As countries think about lifelong learning, secondary education needs to be at the forefront of their minds.

Opening access

Lifelong learning is about giving access to education to individuals from different backgrounds and with different needs. It therefore requires a multiplicity of providers of education and training, offering a multiplicity of modes and settings, and generally also new solutions. I have already noted the major challenges of easy and equitable access and high levels of adult illiteracy in developing countries. Successful ways of including currently excluded populations are needed in developing countries as much as in OECD countries.

The importance of sector-wide, countrywide approaches

The learning society is not just about higher education, or even just about education and training. It is about social relations as well as economics. Former World Bank President James Wolfensohn proposed what he called a Comprehensive Development Framework, which is nothing less than a strategy for a country to develop all of its systems – social, economic, education, etc. – in a coherent and comprehensive way that sees interrelations between them. Such a framework and context for country discussions seems to offer an appropriate forum to talk about lifelong learning.

New ways of learning

OECD countries themselves have far to go in making learning throughout life a reality. It is striking how educational institutions in developed countries still use teaching practices that are rooted in traditional methodologies. Put people in any classroom anywhere in the world and many would be hard-pressed to tell which country they were in, let alone whether they were in the north or the south. In a somewhat perverse way, this gives hope to developing countries, because in this sense they are at the same stage as many developed countries. Indeed, I would venture to suggest that some of the innovations and solutions needed to make lifelong learning a reality in OECD countries may be found in developing countries, in four possible ways. First, in many developing countries there are well-built private education systems with enrolments that are much higher than in OECD countries. This is so for numerous reasons, some good and some not so good. But there may be some lessons to be learned about balancing public and private resources for education. Second, a number of developing countries have experimented with incentives, voucher programmes, tax credits and other innovations to enhance education and training. Third, many developing countries have long experience of using all sorts of technology (not just advanced) to encourage learners and to reach out to otherwise excluded populations. Finally, developing countries have a history of community-based learning, using resources in communities and using communities as a focus for learning activities that go well beyond primary schools – about female health, agricultural practices and so on.

Conclusion

Developing countries have as much interest in what a learning society means as those in the developed world, for all the reasons outlined above.

One point that is often overlooked and not explicitly tackled is the extent to which human contact is important in the learning environment. It is an issue that needs some hard thinking. If we are concerned with the competences and capacities of individuals, it is not immediately apparent that we need to think about human contact. It may be that the only way to learn how to understand others and work in a multicultural environment is by coming together with other people in one place. But there may be other ways of achieving this, and the assumption that all learning must be mediated through person-to-person contact should not be accepted at face value.

Developing countries especially do not have the physical resources to accommodate everybody in classrooms. So even if human contact is the best way of learning, we need to find other effective ways of opening access to learning in situations where human contact is just not possible. What we should not do is question the importance of learning throughout life to the developing world.

Part two
Teaching beyond the boundaries
of formal education:
country responses
to the need for lifelong learning

5. Learning throughout life: an English perspective

Felicity Everiss
Former Head of the Individual Learning
Division for the Department for Education
and Employment in England,
United Kingdom

The intellectual framework for learning throughout life has been well developed at the global level, and philosophical commitment to lifelong learning permeates national social, economic and educational policies. But at the beginning of the new millennium, too little practical lifelong learning has been achieved at any level.

This chapter looks, through English eyes, at some nuts and bolts of implementing lifelong learning policies. It should be stressed that this is an English perspective. There is much common thinking around learning throughout life in the United Kingdom, but policies and their implementation are the responsibilities of separate arrangements in England, Northern Ireland, Scotland and Wales.

We are working towards what is becoming known as 'joined-up government' and 'joined-up' policies – how learning relates to the workplace and the economy, the well-being of the community and society, regeneration and development. Government departments are working together, with varying degrees of success, to co-ordinate their goals, policies and activities.

It is within this framework that England is articulating policies and practices around lifelong learning, broadly defined as 'a "learning society" in which everyone routinely takes up opportunities to learn throughout life'. There is a shared vision – throughout the United Kingdom and in national, regional and local government, in education institutions and companies, within many families and among many individuals – that what we are trying to achieve is learning from the cradle to the grave.

The issues we are tackling involve every level of education, from pre-school to compulsory education (ages 5–16 years), to young people in transition from school to work, to higher education. And, increasingly, learning involves adults in diverse ways, including further education and learning in the workplace, community and family. At many of our universities there are more older people studying part-time than there are young undergraduates.

The word 'learning' is widely used instead of 'education and training', because in the English language 'learning' has a non-value-related meaning: 'education' is perceived by many people to be something academic and 'training' is perceived to be something vocational, while what we are discussing involves all of those kinds of learning and others as well.

Education participation

There are many routes into learning for young and older people, but in the United Kingdom – and indeed in most countries – the older people are, the less likely they are to be involved in learning. This is well illustrated in Figure 1, which shows the percentage of age groups who are participating in learning in formal schooling, higher education, further education or other adult education.

Far more young people than adults are learning, though in the United Kingdom adult participation rates are higher than in most other countries. The table also reveals that the overwhelming majority of people participating in learning are in the formal education sector. This is not surprising, but raises difficult structural and institutional issues that will have to be thought through if genuine efforts are to be made to persuade people to pursue learning throughout life.

Pre-school learning

What does learning from the cradle actually mean? A range of policies has been introduced in England aimed at helping young children get a good start in life, from birth. This entails supporting families and individuals who do not necessarily understand the complexity and implications of economic globalization, technological advance and other aspects of our rapidly changing world.

Fig. 1. Education structure in the United Kingdom

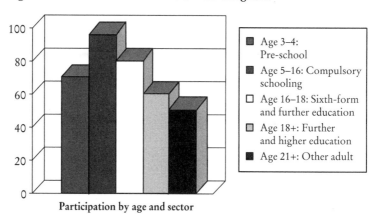

Participation by age and sector

We need to assist individuals to find a place for themselves in a transforming society, nation and world, and to learn how to help their children succeed. An excellent incentive for adult education is to help one's child, and many adults are highly motivated to learn themselves by helping their children. For these reasons, pre-school learning begins with parents.

In England, parents are supported – by health and social services, and the community – from the moment their child is born. The government has put resources into a programme called Sure Start, which is exploring ways of linking the health and social services offered to parents with learning, so that adults can learn with their families and assist their children's early development.

Another programme is aimed at improving early childhood development provision for parents who want to place their children in a learning situation up to the age of 3 or 4, for working reasons or because they believe (as many people do) that learning for part of the day is valuable for the child as well as for the family.

There is also a range of funded projects that are developing partnerships with the voluntary, private and state sectors to expand opportunities for early school places for 3- and 4-year-olds, and child-care arrangements for after school. These programmes are at various stages of development and some are very new, so it is not possible yet to see how well they will work.

But the point is that there is now a strong strategic focus on the early part of life, on the basics of family support and on early learning – all aimed at helping people to get the very best possible start in life as individuals.

Excellence in schools

Within weeks of being elected in May 1997, the United Kingdom's Labour Government produced its first policy document. It covered the second phase in the chronology of educational life and was called *Excellence in Schools*.

It is widely acknowledged that lifelong learning policies and practices depend on getting the basics right: if they are not, governments are not only failing large numbers of people but also neglecting to lay the foundations for later learning. The British Government has focused its education policies around what has been rather controversially called 'zero tolerance of failure'. This does not place blame on children for poor performance. Rather, failure of a child is failure of the education system, the government and society to help that child – this is what we cannot tolerate.

The driving force behind change in education is the goal of excellence. It is about society and the economy, and the way individuals and communities are developed. As the government puts it: 'Educational attainment encourages aspiration and self belief in the next generation – to compete in the global economy, to live in a civilized society and to develop the talents of each and every one of us.'[1] There are six important features of the government's new approach to school learning.

The first is an urgent need for universal literacy and numeracy, the ultimate goal being basic reading-and-writing skills for every person in the country.

Second, there is new emphasis on standards rather than structures, with setting and achieving specific learning targets more important than the way education is currently organized and structured.

Third, there will be state intervention in unsuccessful schools, with intervention inversely related to success. If a school is doing a good job, it will be left alone to get on with it; if it is failing, the government will step in.

Fourth, a range of partnerships are being encouraged, between schools and communities, schools and business, teachers and govern-

1. United Kingdom Department for Education and Employment (DfEE) White Paper, *Excellence in Schools*, July 1997.

ment, teachers and head teachers, pupils and teachers – all with a view to improving standards in education.

Fifth, an experimental programme is underway to create 'education action zones'. The idea is to identify areas and schools where the curriculum is not working and educational performance is relatively poor, and then to try to introduce non-traditional ways of learning and teaching, forming new partnerships between schools, families and communities, and finding innovative ways of improving standards and opening up learning opportunities for people.

Finally, there is a very strong stress on excellent teaching. In many countries, including the United Kingdom, there is a tendency to heap blame on teachers for all educational problems, encouraged by the way politicians speak about and the media reports on teachers. In December 1998 a policy paper was published that changed the tone of the approach to teachers: the Green Paper, *Teachers: Meeting the Challenge of Change*, recognizes the value and professionalism of educators, and supports recognition with the need for better pay and career structures: 'We all need good teachers, whose skills and dedication are recognized and respected. That means a first class profession, well led and well supported. It means backing high standards with high rewards, which recognize the talents of those who teach our children.' But the Green Paper also demands more of teachers in terms of difficult issues such as evaluating performance, modernizing traditional teaching methods that do not always reflect the range of experiences young people have, and using information technologies as a teaching aid and a curricular support. Interest in the Green Paper was intense, with more than 5,000 responses received by the Department for Education and Employment in six weeks.

The learning age

At the end of school individuals move into the 'learning age', which was the name of a discussion document produced in England in February 1998. It discusses all forms of post-compulsory school learning, sketching a broad vision as well as a number of specific initiatives about widening educational participation – not just providing more opportunities, but also for different groups – and sharing responsibility for lifelong learning between national, regional and local government, as well as between individuals and employers.

As with schools, the government's vision of lifelong learning is about society and the economy, the individual, family, culture and community. This is well reflected in *The Learning Age* (DFEE Green Paper, Feb. 1998), which states:

> Learning is the key to prosperity – for each of us as individuals, as well as for the nation. As well as securing our economic future, learning has a wider contribution. It helps make ours a civilized society, develops the spiritual side of our lives and promotes active citizenship. It enables people to play a full part in their community. It strengthens the family, the neighbourhood and consequently the nation.

The United Kingdom is categorized as a developed country, but it has real problems in terms of the levels of learning its citizens have achieved. For a wealthy country it is shocking that: one in four adults have engaged in no deliberate learning in three years; one in four adults have poor literacy and/or numeracy skills; about half of all adults have never touched a computer; 7 million adults have no qualifications; and less learning equals less employment, less pay and poorer health, and makes people less likely to vote.

'Deliberate learning' does not necessarily mean going on a course or formal learning, it is merely setting out to learn something by, for instance, watching television or reading a book. Many British adults have never even been curious about what computers can help them achieve, or about the Internet. There is a great deal of data about lack of learning in the United Kingdom, and there has been much debate about citizenship, democracy and participation in the civic world. What is particularly worrying is that people who do not participate in learning are less likely to vote or participate in civic society: encouraging a learning society has clear implications for effective democracy.

The challenge now is to learn why people do not take part in learning. Generally, we know that individuals want to learn to work to improve their wages and their career prospects, or to help their families (Figure 2). But there is a complicated issue of motivation here, because how is it possible to motivate people to learn if there is a shortage of jobs and difficulty in finding employment, and thus nothing for them at the end of the learning?

Fig. 2. National adult learning survey, 1997

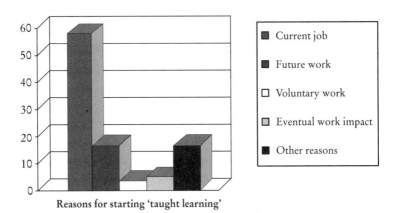

Reasons for starting 'taught learning'

There are less common but significant motivations for learning, such as people wanting to help their community though voluntary work but requiring skills, knowledge and competence to do so. Once entering learning, many people progress via multiple routes into further learning that is relevant to what they do in their working lives or otherwise. There are also many retired people who continue learning, which raises the issues of what learning does for the well-being of the elderly and society, and a possible link between health and learning. If we are genuine about lifelong learning, despite the fact that workers are important in terms of numbers, we have to include people outside the work force – what a colleague calls 'seriously useless learning'. But is it?

Lifelong learning principles

Lifelong learning strategies in England are underpinned by a number of principles: investing to benefit everyone; lifting barriers to learning; putting people first; sharing responsibility; world class standards and value for money; and working together.

These principles are easy to state, far more difficult to put into practice. But they drive lifelong learning as they do schools, and they are about getting learning right for people in the twenty-first century, widening participation and changing priorities regarding who participates – a significant difference lifelong learning policies are trying to make is to expand the diversity of groups involved. There is a need to restructure the system and to dedicate new resources to well-targeted initiatives if problems besetting post-school learning are to be solved and participation widened.

Government overall plans are for:

- Further education growth, with a target of 700,000 more people learning by 2002. New money is being committed to further education so that more – particularly, different kinds of students – can participate.
- A major effort to improve basic skills levels among adults.
- Higher education growth of 100,000 by 2002, with expansion aimed at people from socially disadvantaged backgrounds rather than increasing provision for the middle classes, who have traditionally entered the United Kingdom's very selective system. Universities will obtain money only if they can show they are enrolling people from 'non-traditional' backgrounds.
- Higher standards and quality initiatives. This is about valuing learners and tackling high drop-out rates by improving the standards of teaching and materials.
- Qualifications that are more closely linked to what people are learning and doing, and what is relevant to their lives.
- Partnerships and planning, which concerns sharing resources and working together locally and nationally. A new initiative is bringing local education providers and learners together to look at sharing resources and activities in ways that best meet the needs of the area. Optimal use of resources demands co-operation rather than competition between institutions for students, which is what has been going on for a long time in the United Kingdom.

Investing in young people

The Labour Party promised a number of new lifelong learning initiatives when it was in opposition, which it has subsequently begun delivering. One set of strategies concentrates on young people – what happens in the transition from school to work – and ways of encouraging continuing learning so that young people, including those who directly enter the economy, achieve the qualifications they want and are set on lifelong-learning pathways that enable them to achieve their full potential.

The government has put together a package of programmes aimed at investing in lifelong learning for young people outside the formal tertiary system, including: modern apprenticeships; national traineeships;

the right to study leave for youngsters who begin work but want to carry on learning; education maintenance allowances for young people who need financial support to continue learning; a New Start programme; career guidance to help young people identify learning pathways, both in terms of careers and also covering social and community issues; and a New Deal for the unemployed between the ages of 18 and 24 years.

It is estimated that every year up to 100,000 young people do not follow any route into education, society or the economy after school. There is a key focus on youngsters who seem to disappear off the map (maybe into the black economy or crime), with the idea being to create schemes – vocational, academic or community-based – to put them on the track into mainstream society.

Learning in the workplace

Learning in the workplace is a key area of lifelong learning. The workplace is a natural environment in which to learn, because if you do not you cannot do your job. This is one of the underlying philosophies of lifelong learning. But workplace learning is not just about vocational training for the economic needs of business, significant though that is.

There are a number of initiatives underway to encourage companies to invest in their workforce through lifelong learning. A National Skills Task Force is looking at strategies for the overall development of lifelong learning in the workplace, for instance. And a system of national standards is being created to ensure the quality of workplace learning and its recognition.

To find out what companies are doing to invest in their employees, the government and industry have jointly developed a 'score board' through which it is possible to compare companies in different sectors in terms of their skills investment. Trade unions are becoming increasingly important in the United Kingdom regarding learning approaches to life and work. A trade union learning fund is engaging unions in learning, both within unions themselves and within the industrial structure of the country.

Some companies are involved in employee development schemes that go well beyond their skills requirements and their need to be competitive. The most famous is run by Ford Motors and began in response to labour demands for more learning for employees. As a result a genuinely shared project developed which entitles employees to any kind of learning – from oil painting to playing the flute – rather than just work-related learning. Providing broad learning opportunities has greatly benefited the company in terms of the motivation and morale of employees, and the project has since been extended to include their families.

These kinds of initiatives are being actively encouraged.

The University for Industry

A great deal of interest has been shown in a new government initiative called the University for Industry. UfI is a bit of a misnomer: it is neither a university nor is it for industry. Rather, it is about filling leakages between learners and learning opportunities in the twenty-first century – ensuring that all people are easily able to find the right place of learning for them.

Specifically, UfI aims to drive up demand for learning from individuals, and get supply-side systems organized so that they respond to the needs of individuals. It will massively promote learning and its benefits.

People will be provided with information about what learning opportunities exist, through a free telephone helpline, which is already up and running. Citizens can dial a toll-free telephone number and speak to a qualified adviser able to inform them about all learning opportunities available in the whole country, including England, Scotland, Wales and Northern Ireland. In its first year, the helpline received more than half a million calls, partly because of its heavy promotion through the mass media.

The university will also establish 'local learning centres' country-wide, not by creating new institutions but using existing ones to provide new and different services for learners. Education institutions will be involved in setting up and running learning centres, on their own premises and in libraries, museums, shopping malls and any other places people visit. In the large Gateshead shopping mall in northern England, for instance, there is a partnership venture between education institutions and employers called Learning World, which is always packed with people receiving advice on learning, engaging in learning activities or having their work assessed.

In addition, the University for Industry will commission materials to broaden the range of learning opportunities available countrywide, make wide use of information and communication technologies to support learning, and prioritize the provision of learning opportunities in identified key areas, such as basic skills, information technology and small firms.

The UfI needs to move fast on all these initiatives, since it has the ambitious aim of having around 2 million individuals and companies learning through its system within five to ten years.

Individual learning accounts

Finally, there is a new initiative involving what are called 'learning accounts'. In a nutshell, all adults will be offered financial credit for learning. It is about providing people with an incentive to learn, and about individuals, the government and (hopefully) employers sharing responsibility for funding learning.

This scheme is based on the philosophy underpinning student loans and fees for higher education, which is that individuals gain privately from learning which the government funds but for which it can be repaid at a later, higher-income stage of life. Learning accounts, however, are about spreading public financial investment in post-schooling to all people, enabling individuals to save state 'credits' for learning in which they can participate later in life, when they want to. They are also about garnering support from the government – which has already committed funding to the project for two years – to build over a lifetime a resource that people can draw on to learn.

Specifically, individual learning accounts aim to: (a) increase individual, and hopefully also company, investment in learning; (b) reach 1 million people by 2002 with a public contribution; (c) support learning for people in work; (d) create a national learning framework for all, through financial institutions; and (e) provide incentives to learn.

There are complex issues involved. For instance, financial institutions find it quite difficult to relate broad learning to money. What is the collateral and what, in financial terms, is the value of learning? There is a learner support scheme in England, but the government has to guarantee to banks that it will meet interest costs and failure to repay. The idea of individual learning accounts, however, is more about savings processes and accumulating learning credits for the future.

Targets

It is essential to measure the success of lifelong learning strategies and initiatives. To do so, the government has set a number of targets against which its lifelong learning achievements can be measured. The government's rather risky and ambitious overall targets are, by 2002, to have: two in three 16-year-olds achieve good results in five school-leaving subjects; 85 per cent of 19-year-olds in sixth-form or further education (Level 2); two in three 21-year-olds in further or higher education (Level 3); 28 per cent of adults in further or higher education (Level 3); and 45 per cent of medium to large organizations and 10,000 small organizations who are Investors in People.

Challenges for the future

The government will face many challenges in implementing its lifelong learning strategies, some of which will be very difficult to deal with.

One is the need for cultural change. England has organizations that celebrate learning, learning weeks and campaigns, people telling stories, role models and football clubs promoting learning. But it remains difficult to change people's attitudes to investing in learning, to place equal value on the diverse outcomes of learning and to prioritize some aspects of learning.

Another challenge is public investment priorities. Community and other kinds of learning have very different outcomes and different values attached to them by individuals. A balance between resources channelled into formal education and schools, and ensuring sufficient investment (public, private and individual) in work-based learning is hard to achieve. Finding comprehensive ways to value different kinds of learning, and to fund them fairly, is also very difficult.

It is necessary to demonstrate a rate of return, to justify public expenditure or private investment in various areas of learning and to encourage more money into the system. Setting teaching standards is one way of measuring the quality of learning, which is one return on investment. But hard numbers also need to be attached to the social value of learning. This is not at all the same as demonstrating economic returns, but is essential if a convincing case is to be made for lifelong learning.

A comprehensive system of lifelong learning will require intense collaboration between education institutions that have traditionally been encouraged to compete. Ways will have to be found to persuade institutions which themselves often have tight budgets, to share resources and develop co-operative ways of working together. Capacity for such collaboration still needs to be built.

Finally, there are issues around national control of educational content and curricula, structures, activities and targets, and the growing development of 'bottom-up' educational activity that responds to the needs of local people and areas.

Meeting these fundamental challenges will be a complex task for the whole country as it heads off on the road to lifelong learning for all of its citizens.

6. From virtual campuses to a global campus: a Spanish experience

Francesc Pedró
Professor at the Universitat
Pompeu Fabra, Spain

Our ideas about the role universities are expected to play in society are changing much faster than conceptions about what constitutes a good university education. Opportunities provided by new technologies appear to have been seized by distance universities – or traditional universities embarking on distance education – rather than being used to bring about significant changes to the way people teach and learn at university.

There is something odd about the fact that universities are expected to be responsible for evolving new theories about all kinds of social phenomena, including themselves, yet the pace at which universities are capable of applying those theories reveals a conservative outlook which it is difficult to find in other educational institutions.

The crisis in traditional university teaching and learning

We are witnessing a crisis (in the most ambivalent sense of the term) in all the spheres of knowledge and learning processes in which universities are actively engaged.

On the one hand, the kind of professionals and researchers society expects universities to produce do not have the same profile as those a generation ago. Even in professional and scientific fields in which new technologies have only a minor impact, universities cannot shun the responsibility they bear for training citizens who are skilled in using new technologies and are genuine agents for change and renewal in their fields.

On the other hand, grave doubts are entertained about learning systems that place their trust in transmitting skills through a fragmented picture of professional or scientific knowledge. The compartmentalization of knowledge into subject areas that, like pieces of the children's construction game LEGO, have to fit together in a specific order to obtain a satisfactory final product consistent with the model, makes it difficult to respond to the needs of a new world in which the dominant factors are communication, information handling, problem solving and co-operative works.

Obviously these priorities are not of the slightest value, even in the market, unless they are based on a firm foundation of basic knowledge. But no matter how sound such broad-based knowledge may be, it offers no guarantee that the social and individual expectations placed on university education will be satisfied. Everybody knows that time spent at university, over and above its intrinsic value as a process for acquiring knowledge and skills, has the added value of selecting and shaping society's academically gifted human resources. It has been suggested more than once that degrees awarded to university students are to some extent a less important consideration than the fact of their having succeeded in completing a university course.

However, this observation should not cause us to overlook the importance of renewing university teaching practices in a bid to ensure that students learn more and better in a context increasingly characterized by the growing diversity of their profiles. Accordingly, there is a need for new forms of education that are reflected in new ways of learning and the training of modern professionals. What are these new forms? Why is it so difficult to develop and implement them?

Towards new university teaching models: basic principles

The prime feature of university education is its wide variety of degrees and diplomas, areas of knowledge, subjects and content. This makes it particularly difficult to lay down basic principles that can be applied universally. Even so, it is possible to draw up a common theoretical framework that can guide the processes involved in educational renewal and innovation in universities. Very briefly, this common theoretical framework may be defined by the following basic principles.

First, the prime aim of university education is to provide all-round instruction for people who will develop into high-level professionals or researchers. Often the emphasis placed on the values specific to such all-round instruction yields to pressure to take up a particular discipline. It is necessary to reconstruct university education so that it gives people all-round training, and lays the basis for lifelong learning.

Second, syllabuses should be designed not so much in terms of balanced power-sharing between different subject areas involved in a course of study, but in terms of the final goal being pursued – preparing students to exercise a high-level occupation. This does not mean that traditions associated with certain disciplines should be disregarded: on the contrary, they should be enlisted to cater for the demands of all-round instruction. The aim is not to ensure that students are familiar with the largest possible volume of content in each area or subject, but rather that they progressively acquire the occupational profile for which they are being trained.

Third, this overall trend should be reflected in a review of teaching and learning processes in terms not only of content but also of methods used. As a rule, university-trained professionals are expected to be able to deal with problem solving and with project design, implementation and evaluation. To give students proper training for this purpose, it is necessary to provide a skilful combination of theoretical grounding in a subject and training in problem solving and project development.

Fourth, problem solving and project development require transverse, non-disciplinary skills bound up with communication (written, oral and multimedia), co-operative work (even if done at a distance and not synchronized in time), and especially information handling, irrespective of the medium or place where it is situated. It would be interesting to examine the extent to which these skills are part of the explicit curriculum of universities, or whether they are learned under duress or, as a last resort, held back for postgraduate studies in which academic standards are particularly high.

Fifth, in short, the idea is to shift the focus from teachers, who communicate knowledge, to students, who learn. It is important for lecturers to be able to communicate properly with students, but it is even more important for them to be able to design a high-level learning process that includes knowledge as well as skills and attitudes. From this point of view, considerable effort has to be made to provide vocational training in educational psychology for university teachers.

Finally, stressing students who learn, rather than teachers who teach, means accepting a wide variety of students, who are attending university in greater numbers than a generation ago. We should not necessarily conclude from this that academic standards are now lower than a generation ago – this is a highly debatable point – but rather accept the fact that every student is a unique person who has not only a particular level of knowledge and a distinctive background of training but also unique needs and interests. There is probably no better education, whatever the level involved, than that which is able to provide every individual with as much scope for in-depth study and specialization as necessary, depending on his or her needs.

What makes it so difficult to put these principles into practice? There are probably two main reasons for the complexity involved in applying this theoretical framework. The first is implied in the last two principles, namely the lack of suitable vocational training for lecturers. There are still very few universities offering courses – and these are usually optional – for young lecturers aimed at familiarizing them with crucial aspects of their teaching functions, such as the way adults learn and ways to evaluate learning properly.

The second difficulty is probably of an institutional character and is bound up with the unique and distinctive nature of universities as social institutions engaging in research and teaching. For very different reasons, ranging from their corporate nature to the inertia inherent in large institutions, universities tend to be extremely conservative, especially when they have been designed as a government-funded public service. Changing policies on the relations between governments and universities show, especially in the European countries, that it is necessary to create university funding systems commensurate with expected results, while maintaining and even significantly increasing university autonomy.

Until very recently universities have, on the one hand, tended to act unduly like monopolistic companies that are now beginning to be threatened, and on the other hand, like shopping malls containing various small businesses (departments and the incumbents of professorial chairs) which confine themselves to sharing common costs. In such circumstances it has been very difficult to reform methods of teaching and learning through a common institutional project, which is still something very rare in the public sector. In this field, as in others, existing projects are usually the result of heroic individual endeavours.

New technologies as a window of opportunity

Breakthroughs of new technologies in university education have brought tremendous advantages. Distance universities have generally profited more from the opportunities afforded by new technologies than traditional 'attendance type' universities. But the boundaries separating the two are blurring and the benefits are fast accruing to both.

In reality, introducing new technologies in teaching and learning processes presents a window of opportunity for innovation and the renewal of universities as educational institutions. Indeed, technology breakthroughs are severing the link of physical presence in relations between teachers and students, which is regarded as sacrosanct in some quarters. Even more importantly, any teacher who investigates the scope offered by new technologies to university teaching will have to solve a much more complex task than drawing up a syllabus for the subject he or she teaches. Teachers will have to visualize the goals students will be expected to attain, the activities they should engage in to attain those goals, and above all – this is most crucial for every student – the way their performance should be evaluated.

There would obviously be no point in spending money incorporating technology into university teaching if the final outcome were exactly the same as what could be obtained without the technology. For example, the fact that a good university textbook has already been published should never prompt anyone to convert it unchanged into digital form for publication on the Internet, since students would simply print it out all over again. This risk has to be reckoned with, and can only be handled properly if lecturers are provided with an appropriate framework of educational psychology to enable them to come up with useful strategies.

Universities must press for new technologies to be included in teaching and learning processes, because by doing so in a suitable context of educational psychology they open a window of opportunity for educational renewal and innovation. One of the best and most recent examples of such an opportunity is the creation of virtual campuses the world over.

Virtual campuses as teaching and learning environments

Distance education made extraordinary strides during the past decade. The underlying reasons for growth that is almost unparalleled in the history of distance education are bound up as much with greater demand for education (above all from working professionals) as they are with increased flexibility and speed of communication, coupled with access to digital resources offering new technologies. Universities have not been left out of this general trend. In particular, mature distance universities have witnessed a rush of new projects based on new technologies. These new projects, which share the feature of having a virtual campus, have flourished across continents at a pace faster than educational television. Their success seems undeniable.

A virtual campus may be defined as a learning network that uses digital technology as a connecting medium. In most but not all cases, the main technology used is telematics – a mix of information technology and telecommunications. One of the great advantages of the virtual-campus concept is that, especially when Internet technology is used, students can access the education services of a university at any time and place, can benefit from electronic management and payment mechanisms, and can contact their teachers and fellow students in real time or asynchronously. In short, the idea is to provide permanent access to education for people who would have difficulty gaining it in other ways and with different technologies.

Virtual universities have accordingly been created, with activities primarily centred on creating a virtual environment that facilitates both interpersonal communication and access to services, particularly on-line teaching materials. It is too early to gauge the success of these universities. But it is clearly easier to create a virtual campus as an environment for educational communication than – for very different reasons – to succeed in having high-grade multimedia teaching materials.

Paradoxically, the virtual campus concept makes it much easier for people to communicate with one another than any other system not requiring physical attendance at courses: the level of interaction achieved in a virtual environment may even be greater, in terms of personalization, than what is found in traditional universities under normal conditions. A virtual training environment may make learning more personal because the system has been specifically designed for that purpose. On the other hand traditional university environments, where physical attendance is required, are usually designed on the principle of economies of scale: a teacher gives a lecture simultaneously to a sufficiently large number of students, and the lecture is expected to be understandable enough for there to be little need for interaction at the individual level. Individual attention is largely reserved for post-graduate students, for whom such an investment appears warranted.

Traditional distance universities have been prompted to develop virtual campuses similar to those of new universities that do not require actual attendance. In many cases, especially in 'mega-universities', it is very difficult to change systems, procedures and mental attitudes. However, all distance universities – albeit some more than others – are convinced that they have to build the virtual campus concept into their system and accept all kinds of costs that such transformation may entail.

Lastly, the virtual campus concept has been so successful that it has become the pretext for many traditional universities joining the competition for the distance higher-education market. In some cases, traditional universities have engaged in distance education activities much more speedily than major distance universities have been transforming. This phenomenon was probably predictable in a context in which traditional universities are increasingly being pressured to find new markets, locally and worldwide. It is far easier to access these markets if the virtual campus concept is used, because it is the most suited to breaking down barriers of space and time, at less cost to the institution. Locally, learning flexibility is being sold, while in the global market the commodity is access to internationally prestigious training at minimal cost to students.

It may appear that these developments could have been forecast right from the time that the Internet became accessible and almost indispensable, to the extent that the need to make access to the Internet universal and virtually free of charge has become gospel in some countries. What was less obvious was that intensive use of new technologies in universities would make it possible not only to rethink distance education but also to reframe ideas about what high-quality university education should be in terms of teaching and learning processes.

The global campus concept as a salutary lesson

It is in this context that new departures such as the global campus take on their full meaning. In fact, the idea is to reformulate the concept of university education by combining the advantages of traditional campuses with those of virtual campuses, while taking into account that both are being enlisted in the service of training all teaching bodies. The potentials of traditional and virtual universities have to be combined to derive the utmost benefit from both, keeping in mind that the main focus should be on the activities of students in a co-operative work context. Thus, for example, the main resource on a traditional campus is individual members of the teaching body, while the main resource on a virtual campus is remote and asynchronous access to equipment, services and people. If the goal is to train people in all their varied facets, a global approach has to be adopted: attendance type and asynchronous opportunities must be combined in a single programme.

Such a theoretical formulation may appear straightforward. But applying the idea runs into countless problems of all kinds, ranging from technological infrastructures and investment in a technologically competent population within university precincts – with constant upgrading – to acceptance by the teaching body of a project that can succeed only if teachers are committed to it. The acceptance of teachers is bound to depend on their having a proper grasp of the enormous scope a combined environment can afford university education.

In an environment like the global campus all the members of the teaching staff, properly supported by other professionals and technical experts (computer engineers, educational psychologists, librarians and so on) have to become not only depositories of knowledge that they are required to transmit orally through lectures, but also managers in the extremely complicated processes involved in training students. In this context training management or engineering – what was merely called teaching a few years ago – is defined as being the design of training processes; planning and scheduling of objectives; use of materials and all available resources (starting with individual teachers and including the scope offered by connecting with other universities); supervision of the process; and, lastly, its evaluation and appropriate accreditation – in short, the whole teaching/learning operation.

New objectives for university training

Relations between society and universities have always been strained, marked either by their subordination to social needs and the established social order or by an often naïve belief in the university as a unique mechanism for far-reaching social reform. It is odd to note how, until now, these relations have evolved in a framework based on the assumption that there was going to be no radical change in society in the following generation. Today, relations between society and universities are even more strained, compounded by the conviction that the future of society is more open-ended than ever and thus more uncertain.

It is against this background of uncertainty that there looms the prospect of the information society as a new social model, in which people work, engage in business, communicate and learn on electronic networks – and live on them, too. In view of the rate at which networks are growing, it is difficult to deny that prospects for today's university students are shaped by the information society, with the truly hectic pace of change it involves in all spheres of life, from work to inter-personal relationships to cultural identities. It is a pace of change that requires application of the principle of lifelong learning as the only possible response.

What will the goals of university education be in this new context, and what role can technology play in achieving these goals?

The university of the information society

The following four new goals can be added to long-standing principles governing education and universities: (a) making technology trans-parent; (b) paving the way for dual citizenship; (c) ensuring that people are included by technology; and (d) recreating cultural identities.

Making technology transparent

Technology can be regarded as a tool with huge potential. As such, the prime objective of university education should be to ensure that technology is transparent – it should be made into a tool that students do not see but which they use, because it is not so much the tool that draws their attention as the use to which they put it, and above all the purpose for which they intend using it. For most students a ballpoint pen, as a piece of technology, is transparent: they know how to use it, and when they hold it in their hands they do not concentrate on its shape or mechanism but on what they want to express when they write or draw. If the pen does not work they look for another, not bothering about its colour or shape so long as it allows them to carry on writing or drawing. If, on the other hand, they had the controls of a glider in mid-flight in their hands rather than a ballpoint pen, they would concentrate on discovering how the controls work and making them work in time.

Consequently, it is clear that universities must contribute to work done by other educational actors by bearing their share of respon-sibility in the following two new areas:

- Preparing people to use technologies, not only in the sphere of necessary instrumental skills – which may change as technological innovation changes – but also to adopt strategies for communicating and working with information in a networked digital medium.
- Preparing for the application, in personal terms, of the principle of education throughout life, most probably with due regard to the fact that technology will become a key tool for obtaining flexible and open-ended access to training at any time and in any place, at the student's chosen pace.

The best way of contributing to this objective is to provide students with appropriate training opportunities. In other words, it is advisable to supplement an objective that has always been easy to grasp – such as learning to use a particular technology – with two more objectives that are much more closely concerned with the purpose to which that usage is put, namely communication and work with information, and the ability to access more information through technology.

Paving the way for dual citizenship

In present circumstances university students, no matter which country they are from, represent the core population best placed to be in the vanguard of efforts to confront social challenges raised by the information society. One of these challenges lies in the new meaning of the concept of citizenship, to be found in a social model that exists both in physical and virtual reality. In educational terms, this means that universities should adopt the following two new objectives:

- Preparing students to apply the values inherent in citizenship in a democratic society to communication and life on networks. In other words, learning the ethics of virtual citizenship as a new dimension of the ethics of democratic citizenship. In future, it is very likely that this task will begin in schools.
- Preparing people to use technology as a tool to give added depth to life in a democracy, by examining the scope for participation and, more generally, for processes of governance and administration in the information society.

Ensuring that people are included by means of technology

Everyone knows that in university education, which already occupies a special place worldwide, the pressing need to use new technologies intensively may help make it possible to bridge gaps between different social strata within and between different countries and regions the world over. Paradoxically, the only way to avoid such gaps is to do away with them altogether, either by forgoing the use of technology or by making technology a precious ally in combating social exclusion. Even though the idea of introducing technology into areas where there are a great many shortages may seem inappropriate or objectionable, lack of technology in those areas cannot be made into yet another shortage. On the contrary, offsetting formulae of various kinds will have to be applied, such as:

- International co-operation in respect of transfers of technology and know-how.
- International co-operation around a new global university or network university concept. It would be unpardonable not to use new technologies as a resource against geographical, economic and social constraints. Such international co-operation could be very rewarding in such hitherto unexplored areas as virtual mobility: in other words, affording remote access to university courses given at any institution in the world, wherever students may be, or providing increasing numbers of population categories with access to the benefits of higher education.
- Using technologies as tools of social inclusion. What is needed in this area is a stronger dose of creativity, innovative experiment research.

Re-creating cultural identities

The last and particularly significant objective is cultural identities. Everybody is conscious that, inasmuch as the information society is a society made up of networks, it is likely that the largest supplier of technology networks and content will become the prime standard of reference and, ultimately, the dominant culture. A new culture may also be created partly from the most distinctive features of a dominant culture, and partly from other new features, as if a sort of global culture were involved, capable of absorbing local cultures. In a context in which people's lives will be lived on the Internet, if a local culture does not succeed in making its presence known on the short-term network, it may disappear as a genuine culture. There is an urgent need to develop a process in which cultural entities can be re-created, in a bid to make way for this fresh dimension, which is different from cultural identity proper.

It is along these lines that universities should become key tools for re-creating cultural entities. It is accordingly very important for them:

- To exercise control over tools used in creating and enjoying culture, including culture in the digital medium.
- To situate a culture's own identity in the broader context of the Internet and of the relations that develop between different cultures.

The real potential of new technologies in university education

Over and above the demands arising out of the information society concept in terms of redefining or updating university training processes, the technologies involved appear also to have potential as tools for improving the quality – and probably the quantity – of university education. It must be asked whether new technologies supply added value not only to the content of university education but also to the quality of the processes involved. It is in this area that there are conflicting views on what university education really is.

New technologies provide universities, and other levels of education, with at least two novel features:

- Access to a much larger volume of information and to multimedia, a new medium whose main feature, in theory, is a high degree of interactivity and flexibility.
- Communication, by means of instant connections, with other people in other universities and other contexts.

There is no need to stress that these two factors alone are genuine innovations compared, on the one hand, with the medium of educational content, and on the other hand with the possibility of interchange and communication. They are new resources that have been entrusted to teachers. Yet there is something to be said about the idea that technologies can be used in universities and lecture halls without necessarily improving the quality of learning delivered in situations where such technologies do not exist.

An example is the conventional university lecture hall, where the teacher is the student's only opposite number and where the teacher assigns textbooks and notes. The ultimate reason for this model is economic: the utmost advantage should be taken of a very limited and costly resource – the university teacher – and economies of scale are obtained by filling lecture halls with large numbers of students.

However, referring to the potential of new technologies to widen access to such a valuable resource (and achieve greater economies of scale) without also referring to the capacity they offer, when used properly, to improve teaching and learning processes, is missing the point. New technologies are not just one more educational resource, albeit a highly valuable one, but a salutary lesson that teaches us to rethink the university system as a whole as well as what goes on in the lecture room, starting with the way such activity is organized from the inside and the relationships established, particularly between teachers and students.

It is possible to imagine a situation in which all students have a computer that, even if not a new model, connects to the Internet, the rest of the university and the world at large. This would provide all students with a new working tool with which they could access large number of facts and resources inside and outside the university, as well as being able to communicate with people in any part of the world. In such circumstances, we would conclude that traditional methods of teaching and learning would have to be overhauled to derive maximum benefit from them.

In this perfectly conceivable situation, a university teacher would govern a process that is much more complex, but more focused on the active work of the student, whether he or she is working alone or in co-operation with other students. The assumption is that it is much easier in this new scenario to give individual attention to each student because teachers can devote some of the time they used to spend on verbal explanations to follow up individual students' work.

All in all, this new situation calls for reconsideration of the teacher's function. This is beyond the scope of this chapter. However, estimates have been made of the percentages of time university teachers currently devote to the various tasks they perform, and the percentages they would probably devote to them if their students had access to technology on campus, at home or in a public service or institution. It is easy to calculate how much time teachers can save by reducing the presentation of their subjects. But new technologies also point to a considerable increase in the scope teachers have for preparing lectures, clearing up doubts and ensuring personal follow up.

There appear to be only two obstacles to a scenario such as this. The first is economic – defrayal of the requisite capital and recurrent costs. The other is pedagogical – the availability of teaching staff who are trained to make the most of new technologies and are utterly convinced of the improvements they imply. Neither obstacle is insurmountable, but the gaps between dreams and reality are very wide. This situation, rather than any other, is what distinguishes the university of the information society.

Conclusions and recommendations

It would currently be very difficult to accept any country's claim that its education and university systems are those of the information society. This is still wishful thinking, but not necessarily in the realm of Utopia. Even in countries where nearly 90 per cent of university students are said to use the Internet every day, the university system continues to be based on the traditional model, subject to the addition of technologies with varying degrees of success.

It is also difficult, in such circumstances, to regard the role of universities as noteworthy in terms of configuring a new model of society. On the contrary, there are indications that the image young university students have of the information society is more influenced by their experiences of cinema, television and computer games. More-over, analysis of these images has shown that young students are perfectly able to distinguish between serious and boring applications – which are reserved for adults, the world of work and some cases for work in particular areas – and other applications that are much more interesting because they offer different experiences and sensations, and in which they are the main actors. This double view of things is worrying to say the least.

If the information society is one in which people live and learn with technologies, then the university of the information society should make it possible to live from day to day and also to learn through technologies. It is not easy to do this: first, it is necessary to bring into play a set of factors that will give a new lease of life to universities and the rules governing them.

Purely for guidance purposes, the following recommendations could be borne in mind. Preparing for the information society is bound to be of a transverse nature. It is not advisable to focus preparation on a single subject or set of subjects or a clearly defined context, because emphasis would then be placed on learning the technology rather than on the purposes for which it is used and its transfer to different contexts.

Indeed, if such a transfer is to be possible, greater importance needs to be attached to project work and emphasis reduced on breakdown by subjects. At the same time, it is essential to create real university-type teaching practices.

To further this aim, it is essential to change university space and time dimensions. In other words, it is important for universities to develop structural approaches and transferable practices that enable learning to be focused on the student's work rather than on the teacher's lectures. Regarding the time factor, it is also necessary to do away with the rigidity of over-fragmented timetables. The complex nature of knowledge and interdisciplinary work do not tally very well with classes lasting fifty minutes.

One fundamental feature of the information society is the potential it offers for remote access to information. This being the case, it is essential to ensure that all universities are interconnected. This is coming to be known as the global or network university.

In future, teachers will continue to be the most important actors in university education. If more is required of them, they must be given more, in the broadest sense of the term. Different ways should be found to ensure that all teachers share commitment to the information society, and have the human and technical capacity to reflect that commitment in different ways, depending on the individual context. With this in mind, information technologies and products must be as open-ended as possible, in a bid to ensure that adapting these products to the tangible needs and, where possible, individual needs of students ultimately depends on the teachers.

In these circumstances, it is crucial to begin setting up procedures and methods for the initial and lifelong training of university teachers in those aspects of new technologies that are most closely bound up with teaching practices. Similarly, teaching practices should set the example when it comes to using new technologies.

In this complex process, geared to contributing to the emergence of the information society, it is the duty of universities – in accordance with the mission they have performed from the outset – to open up paths along which other formal education institutions will eventually also have to pass. In this undertaking, universities of the future may well bear little resemblance to those we have known in the past. If we still call them universities, it will undoubtedly be because they continue to be passionately involved in research and the spread of knowledge.

7. Learning throughout life: a Latin American perspective[1]

María de Ibarrola
Research Professor in the Department
of Educational Research at the Centre
of Research and Advanced Studies,
Instituto Politécnico Nacional (IPN)
in Mexico City

Learning throughout life is not just a fashionable slogan. It is a cultural, sociological, pedagogical and psychological proven fact – learning takes place through every additional human experience. What is new is recognition, in a rapidly changing world, that learning throughout life must be a priority of cultural, social and economic policies.

Four major issues oblige us to be interested in lifelong learning. First, societies are facing profound changes, and will continue to do so for years to come. Second, there are serious questions around whether the kind of learning opportunities people have had enable them to face these changes. Third, there is a major debate about what the main goals of lifelong education are, and what it ought to achieve. Finally, we have to define who is responsible for national and international lifelong learning policies.

The nature of change

The last three decades of the twentieth century anticipated the intensive changes humanity now faces: globalization of economies, ever faster technological development, and deep political and cultural transformation. These changes are not following a single trend. On the

1. This chapter is based on a paper, presented by the author at the second International Colloquium, 'Education in the Twenty-first Century', hosted by the Mexican Foundation of Academic Exchange in Mexico City, November 1998.

contrary, they are detonating complex, conflicting processes within and between countries, processes linked to each other through dynamics that tend to widen the distance between their different results.

There are four main economic trends. The first is changes in the labour market, and it can be organized around six central issues: the need to develop workers' qualifications to meet the challenges of a transforming job market; changes in workers' careers, which will be dominated by uncertainty; a general tendency to increase services and reduce primary and secondary activities; new working conditions that lean more towards team and collective work than hierarchical organization of production; new relations among enterprises which can be built around their common tendencies: outsourcing, downsizing and re-engineering; and new rules regarding labour rights. As regards the final issue, there is an erosion of what used to be social responsibility towards workers in terms of their rights to a stable and permanent job, guaranteed minimum wages, good conditions, set working hours and fringe benefits.

A second trend is the growth of work in the informal labour market, where conditions are often very difficult. Third is the creation of different kind of jobs outside the market in what is known as the 'third', 'solidarity' or 'social' sector. The fourth trend is the total exclusion from economic activities of large sectors of the population who simply do not work (Novick and Gallart, 1997; Gitahy, 1994).

Technological advancement risks destroying our planet. Societies face a triple challenge in trying to control this tendency: first, the need for a critical mass of people able to understand and direct the implementation and use of advanced technologies for general democratic human well-being and ecological preservation; second, the need for innovative groups able to reorient comprehension and development of technology in order to solve ancient production and organizational problems that have been an obstacle to progress until now in many countries; and, third, a basic technological culture for everyone is needed to exert democratic pressure on technological developments so as to prevent repetition of the horrific problems that technological advances have caused both in developed and developing countries, but especially in less developed countries. The irresponsible use of technology has put human life at risk, caused ecological destruction, helped concentrate wealth in the hands of a few and increased extreme poverty.

Political change centres on the need for a new citizenry who actively participate and have a role in decision making for democratic and general human development. Political decision making involves increasingly complex technical and ethical considerations which must be taken into account. There is also a need in every country to redefine the basis of representation and the legitimacy of political leaders, and to redefine individual human rights in view of collective rights.

Cultural changes are visible in the priority that concepts like cultural pluralism, diversity and respect for differences have acquired, and in the emergence of all sorts of discrimination – by gender, age, religion, ethnicity, language, nationalism and so on – being expressed in most countries, sometimes violently and sometimes with extreme fundamentalism.

In the face of these profound changes and the economical, political and cultural challenges they pose, three main demographic trends need to be taken into consideration. The first is women's participation in the labour force and public life, which is radically transforming the traditional roles of women. On the one hand, this has caused deep role conflicts and on the other, the devaluation of wages and labour conditions in sectors where women are in the majority. The second is the change in the balance between productive and unproductive life. As life expectancies increase for almost everybody due to medical discoveries and health policies, adults face early retirement which leaves them with fifteen to twenty years of healthy life without social or economic incorporation. Also, young people tend to reach formal employment later. The productive life-span often now lasts no more than twenty years, between the ages of 30 and 50, generating a far greater burden of unproductive people to care for. The third is labour-force migration, which, within and between countries, is already affecting millions of people. Migrant groups are often excluded from many public services: basic labour rights and fringe benefits, health, social security and education. Migration movements have changed since the 1950s, and tend to impact on both recipient and expelling countries in terms of cultural diversity and economic inequality.

Future changes can be expected to be multiple, different and unequal. Trends show us that changes are occurring at the same time, both within and between countries.

There is an optimistic scenario based on an exclusive vision of technological advance and a resulting magnitude of wealth and productivity. In this scenario, economic transformation is dynamic and is gradually but strongly incorporating a variety of enterprises, even rural and traditional ones. Lifelong education is needed to prepare young people and adults for continuous change.

There is also a pessimistic scenario, where labour policies have to choose between a model in which a few people are employed while the rest live on public welfare, or a model in which more people work for fewer hours or days. In both cases, the result is more free time, making lifelong education necessary for people to benefit personally and collectively from new recreational time (Aaronowitz and DiFazio, 1994; Rifkin, 1995).

A third, much needed understanding of the future arises from actual conditions of extreme poverty, huge inequality and economic, political and social exclusion for many sectors of the population in most Latin American countries. Trends have to be seen from a different perspective. Unlike in developed countries, formal employment is often the exception. Poor and precarious working conditions – those most feared in the pessimistic scenario – are the rule for most rural and urban marginal workers in Latin America. The concept of 'free time' acquires a different connotation. People do not have leisure time: rather, they spend many inefficient hours a day waiting for an opportunity to earn a minimal income or to complete cumbersome tasks. The need is for basic education, understood as first-chance educational opportunities, rather than for continuing education, often understood in terms of lifelong learning. Access to literacy, numeracy, education and information still has a vital role in helping to meet fundamental needs in Latin America.

Lifelong learning and the need for new basic competences

These social, economic, cultural and political changes demand new basic knowledge, skills and practices. Most Latin American countries have undertaken profound educational reforms in order to achieve them, including longer basic education (nine to ten compulsory years), curricular change, decentralization of school management, more social participation in education and demands for school accountability.

Literacy is perhaps the most basic practice where deep new change is visible. Previously, an internationally accepted literacy measure was the ability to read and write a simple family or business letter, an address or a transport schedule, or even recognize and write one's own name. New literacy demands the ability to read and comprehend complex technical orders, follow instructions in handbooks, fill out forms at work or for civil business, or at least read and understand risk warnings (such as seeds not fit for human consumption). People are required to understand the logic of mass media, or risk manipulation, to understand the language of computers, to use more than one language and ever more frequently to use an international lingua franca (English). Without this kind of literacy, people tend to be excluded from economic and cultural globalization.

Similar arguments can be put forward regarding mathematics and natural sciences. We can also justify the need for new basic knowledge in social sciences: geography, for instance, can be a major economic device. History, the humanities and ethics are indispensable for self-appraisal, cultural integration and valuing the consequences of human decisions, especially the implications of technological development, such as the risks involved in nuclear energy. All societies need a new basic technological literacy. While technology invades daily life in most corners of the world, knowledge and understanding of its basic mechanisms are lacking in large segments of populations, who are therefore unable to prevent, oppose or control its risks (de Ibarrola and Gallart, 1994).

We have to understand that the role of the school system is irreplaceable in acquiring these basic competences. In most countries in Latin America, there is still a high illiteracy rate – a mean of 15 per cent of adults, measured in the traditional way. It is far higher if measured as defined above. Most people have not acquired even six years of schooling in some countries, and very few youngsters stay on at school beyond the age of 14 or 15 years.

Basic education has proved to be extremely unequal, insufficient and inefficient for important population sectors. In Mexico, for instance, around 1.5 million children aged between 6 and 14 are out of school, and only 54 per cent of those who start school actually finish compulsory Grade 9 education. Nearly 14 million youngsters aged between 15 and 24 are out of school, and less than 17 per cent of that age-group achieve a higher education. Adult education is mostly oriented towards elementary literacy programmes and primary schooling. Adults who want more appealing opportunities for learning struggle to find them. Even in countries where on-the-job training is compulsory, actual opportunities are very rare.

We cannot underestimate the different and unequal points of

departure for most sectors of the population, which determine their actual potential to benefit from lifelong learning. A major problem seems to be the large number of adolescents and young adults with only a few years of inadequate schooling, who are not eligible for adult literacy or employment programmes and have no jobs. Experts estimate that some 5 million youngsters are effectively excluded from both education and work in Latin American countries (Jacinto, 1998). Secondary education, therefore, becomes a major priority, but has been neglected during educational reforms (de Ibarrola, 1996).

In the face of these realities it is not easy to blithely recommend learning beyond school. Major changes within school systems are already being carried out in many countries, for instance the Escuela Nueva community courses, Tele Secundaria and open systems. Before abandoning school policies, we need to exhaust the potential of a school pedagogical Utopia and achieve the preconditions for lifelong learning. Basic competences are acquired through a daily effort to create learning practices and abilities, daily exposure to comprehensible knowledge and understanding of people's rich and different cultures, and daily development of human potential. There need to be daily efforts to read and write in multiple and meaningful ways, and daily interactions among young people and qualified adults around scientific knowledge aimed at fostering the overall development of every child. For all this, there is still no substitute for the school system. A huge effort needs to be poured into secondary education in most Latin American countries.

Poor educational results do not justify abandoning school policies, because they come as no surprise after analysing national educational policies in many Latin American countries. Despite a century of effort (mostly declarations) education budgets have been proportionally lower than those even of less developed countries in Asia and Africa. Yet school enrolments, drop-out rates and repetition have ceaselessly grown. This paradox has been caused, among other things, by poor teacher training, low salaries and difficult working conditions, lack of basic materials, too little time devoted to learning and double shifts for teachers and schools.

Extra lifelong-learning priorities are not the solution to unfilled basic education needs and they certainly cannot be a substitute. Learning throughout life cannot be understood without the strong basic education that prepares people to learn efficiently from new opportunities and daily experiences. Research and experience show that self-teaching is a complex process and is rarely found among non-qualified or illiterate people. Those who profit from updating and upgrading learning, for instance, tend to be people with higher qualifications to begin with.

Basic learning competence is crucial to taking advantage of new learning opportunities, both in order to advance in the psychological process of learning, and to strengthen and broaden personal knowledge structures, and in order to be able to choose wisely from among the ever-growing number and kind of educational opportunities opening up. On the other hand, the responsibility for creating and conducting innovative, efficient, quality lifelong learning can only be undertaken by a critical mass of highly educated people in every country.

Indeed, technological development has brought many new learning opportunities, especially through telecommunications and personal computers, and the infinite resources that can be accessed via them. Developed societies have been able to organize learning communities, even develop the concept of 'educational cities' in which every citizen can find multiple learning options that are easily accessible in terms of adapting to individual learning interests and abilities, payment alternatives, times, response to job demands and so on. This is simply not the case in less developed countries, where basic school is the only learning opportunity for many communities.

Lifelong learning policies: where to from here?

Lifelong learning has featured in the educational policies of most Latin American countries for at least five decades. Continuous professional updating is perhaps the most visible example, found in permanent education programmes at universities. Another example, in many countries, is workers being legally entitled to compulsory training. What is new is the realization of the need for constantly changing competences, and for education throughout life for all – for cultural, political and economic reasons. The only solution proposed for this is learning to learn (CEPAL-UNESCO, 1992; European Commission, 1995; Delors et al., 1996).

The end point should be a learning society in which every person can easily join a learning spiral that encourages cultural, political and economic inclusion, a spiral that starts with basic schooling. Societies can reach this educational state only when they are able to tackle five main challenges by:

- Directing financial resources and creative energy towards new basic school opportunities, especially for youngsters, and towards flexible, accessible lifelong learning opportunities.

- Promoting a wide range of different opportunities that can answer a multiplicity of needs and guarantee equitable opportunities for all. Social recognition of learning – market recognition and public certification – stands amid a tension between diversity and equity, and is currently very important, embodied in certification standards and criteria and fostered by both national and international groups, particularly regarding the labour market.

- Transforming learning opportunities in response to new external social, economic and cultural dynamics, versus the time needed to consolidate new institutions and organizations offering lifelong education. The most important issue is consolidating the qualifications of those who will be responsible for teaching in a context of pluralism, diversity, continuous change and the organization of new information resources. It is a social fact that activities have to be institutionalized, at least minimally, in order to meet their goals, social functions, resources, organization and need for accountability efficiently. A major problem in Latin America is the precariousness of new education opportunities.

- Achieving and certifying learning that opens up real new opportunities, as opposed to the currently restricted opportunities to use or profit from knowledge acquired, derived from adverse work or social organization and conditions. Workplaces are good examples of this contradiction: it is easier to offer courses to workers than to promote them or pay better wages.

- Orienting education opportunities towards enabling social groups to adapt to the many and varied demands of globalization, versus the innovation and transformation of goals that seems already to be needed in order to redefine the objectives of social, economic and cultural transformation despite the enormous speed of change and precisely so as to close the distance between antagonizing processes.

Responsibility for lifelong learning policies

Education throughout life – intended to provide all people with the basic knowledge and skills needed to learn to learn, and the opportunities to do so throughout life – is a public matter. It cannot be reduced to a market dynamic that emphasizes either the demand or the supply of lifelong-education opportunities. Both actual demand and actual opportunities offered are insufficient for the goals we propose.

Demand itself can be analysed from several perspectives: (a) the reduced or non-existent capacity of many groups to demand opportunities; (b) the meaning and orientation of precise demands as regards local, regional, national and international educational needs; or (c) the resources allocated to meet demands. Experience shows that people with more schooling and income tend to have the greatest capacity to exert pressure for educational opportunities.

Supply, too, can be seen from different points of view. First, most lifelong-learning chances are channelled through schools that lack relationships with other sectors of society, precisely because they have long suffered from the speed of change versus the time they need to transform internally and adapt their functions to new demands. Second, many social institutions crucial to lifelong learning have not accepted responsibility for it, especially in developing countries – the mass media are a case in point. Third, international electronic networks are inaccessible to many sectors in developing countries.

Important questions to ask are: Who is responsible for the lifelong learning of young people who have insufficient schooling and who are already excluded from educational and working opportunities? Who is responsible for the lifelong education of workers in the informal labour market? Who is responsible for the lifelong learning of adults whose life expectancy is much longer than the years they will spend in the labour force? Who is responsible for the civic education of communities interested in complex local decision making, such as the construction of a petrol-filling station in their area? Who is responsible for the cultural integration of migrant groups? Many of these needs have not yet reached the point of demand.

These examples lead us to public responsibility for learning policies.

But public and private definitions are also changing. We cannot reduce public activities to government or private enterprises to profit. There is an interesting mix of public–private interactions. New social actors are appearing, and there are new ways of developing policies and programmes that involve public and private entities. Fund-raising and the distribution of financial resources involve fiscal resources and private management. Accountability and evaluation have to be extended to private groups, not only to government actors.

Incorporating everyone into an inclusive learning spiral calls for different educational circles, but diversity also requires public co-ordination if it is to resolve tensions inherent in today's world. Democracy, as the basis for effective public co-ordination, is both a requirement and a consequence of such public policies.

International co-operation has to reach a balance between understanding basic educational needs in different countries and promoting new educational trends. International co-operation has to take fully into consideration that the priority of lifelong learning policies in countries where basic education needs have long been satisfied, cannot be exported without perverse effects on countries where basic schooling for all is still a distant dream.

References

Aaronowitz, S.; DiFazio, W. 1994. *The Jobless Future*. Minneapolis, University of Minnesota Press.

CEPAL-UNESCO. 1992. *Educación y Conocimiento. Eje de la transformación productiva con equidad* [Education and Knowledge: Basic Pillars of Changing Production Patterns with Social Equity], Santiago de Chile, CEPAL/UNESCO.

De Ibarrola, M. 1996. Seven Fundamental Policies for Secondary Education in Latin America: Current Situation and Prospects). Meeting of Ministers of Education from Latin America and the Caribbean, Jamaica, May 1996.

De Ibarrola, M.; Gallart, M. A. (eds.). 1994. *Democracia y productividad. Desafíos para una nueva educación media en América Latina* [Democracy and Productivity: Challenges for a New Media Education in Latin America]. Santiago, Buenos Aires/Mexico City, OREALC-UNESCO. Red Latinoamericana de Educación y Trabajo.

Delors J., et al. 1996. *Learning: The Treasure Within. Report to UNESCO of the International Commission on Education for the Twenty-first Century*. Paris, UNESCO Publishing.

European Commission. 1995. *Teaching and Learning: Towards the Cognitive Society*. (White Paper on education and training.) Brussels, European Commission.

Gitahy, L. 1994. *Reestructuración productiva, trabajo y educación en América Latina* [Restructuring Productivity, Work and Education in Latin America]. CIID-CENEP. Red Latinoamericana de Educación y Trabajo, Cinterfor ILO, UNESCO-OREALC, UNICAMP.

Jacinto, C. 1998. *Formación para el trabajo de jóvenes de sectores de pobreza de América Latina. Qué desafíos, qué estrategias* [Job Training for Young People from Deprived Areas of Latin America: What are the Challenges, What are the Strategies?]. Bogotá.

Novick, M.; Gallart, M. A. (eds.). 1997. *Competitividad, redes productivas y competencias laborales* [Competitiveness, Productivity and Labour Competences]. Cinterfor-ILO, Red Latinoamericana de Educación y Trabajo.

Rifkin, J. 1995. *The End of Work*. New York, Putnam.

8. Societies in transition: a South African case-study

Enver Motala
Educational consultant to South Africa's
national and provincial governments.
Senior official from 1994 to 1997
in the Gauteng Province
Department of Education

Different societies face different challenges in developing and applying appropriate lifelong learning strategies. Experience of learning throughout life has been documented mainly in stable and affluent societies.

Three crucial issues confront transitional societies such as those in Africa, Latin America and Eastern Europe and have an impact, *inter alia,* on the ability of governments to provide lifelong learning opportunities for their citizens.

The first is the question of how they ought to deal with problems of development. More than a decade after the end of the Cold War and the global embrace of democracy and market economics, little is understood about the nature of transitional societies and their particular developmental challenges.

The second is a disjuncture between policy and practice in all transitional societies. High popular expectations of what political transition will deliver place major, cumulative demands on the nation-state. The response is a flurry of political activity but not necessarily much change on the ground. Change needs to be carefully managed, and experience gained of transition so far is that change must be incremental. Key target areas need to be identified, rather than attempts being made to solve all problems at once. If, for example, it is thought that the best way to transmit knowledge to millions of people who have previously been disadvantaged is through the use of innovative media, that is where efforts should be heavily focused.

The third and most worrisome issue flows from a rapidly global-izing environment that has undermined the role of nation-states. There has been a shift in attitudes back to acknowledging the importance of governments by, for instance, the World Bank after the South-East Asian economic crisis and financial market instability of 1998. In poor countries, especially those ridden by inequalities, the state is often the only mechanism available to protect sovereignty, to overcome histor-ical deficits and encourage even development. Market forces alone have been shown to be inadequate in ensuring equitable development – indeed, they have increased inequality.

The comments that follow in this chapter are based on the South African experience: their relevance to other countries cannot be assumed, because of the specificity of South African circumstances. The general conclusions drawn may not be directly applicable to other developing contexts, notwithstanding the obvious imprint of globaliz-ation on all developing countries – for instance, the effects of trade and tariff policies, financial regimes, changes in production systems, labour standards and, most important, transgressions against the sovereignty of nation-states. This chapter attempts to contextualize the transition to democracy in South Africa, and to raise questions about the nature of the process of transition and reform, especially in relation to questions about education and training, policy and practice.

Policy and practice

Immediately after transition to democracy in April 1994, South Africa's new African National Congress-led Government began producing a constellation of policy documents. From comments made by external consultants and participants in the policy process in South Africa, it can probably be said that there has never been an array of documents of the kind and weight produced in any other comparative experience. South Africa has legislation on every single matter, white papers, green papers, discussion documents, new regulatory frameworks – all, of course, driven by massive consultative processes undertaken in the years after democracy was achieved, and in some cases before the ANC came to government.

Current policy propositions attempt to address fundamental problems such as equity, redress, access, quality and relevance – the very issues with which so many countries are grappling – through policies of lifelong learning. A reading of these documents reflects the language and the need for flexible learning systems, all found in the international education discourse.

Education policies are intended to form frameworks for innovative development strategies for South Africa. More specific strategies that have flowed from these broad policy parameters relate in particular to making lifelong learning possible: a national curricular framework, recognition of prior learning, flexible and open learning systems, and new learning organizations. Very important has been the integration of education with vocational training, to demystify the academic and upgrade the vocational, with stress on the concept of critical learning.

Education is managed by provincial governments, with the national government responsible for overall policies, and setting national norms and standards – South Africa's nine provinces have set up institutes for lifelong learning.

The South African Qualifications Authority (SAQA) has been established, responsible for creating a National Qualifications Framework (NQF) based on the principles of outcomes-based education. Eventually all South African courses will be credited by SAQA agencies and qualifications at all levels, from school to postgraduate degrees, will slot into a framework aimed at ensuring standards and enhancing educational access, flexibility and mobility. A new outcomes-based curriculum, called Curriculum 2005, is being phased into schools and is intended to spur South Africa into modernity and international competitiveness.

We have a new Skills Development Act and a skills levy on private-sector payrolls aimed at encouraging workplace and lifelong learning, and at funding training for the unemployed. Sector education and training authorities are being formally established by the Department of Labour, their mandate being to promote human-resource development and lifelong learning in every sector of the economy. Greater participation in the education system has been encouraged through educational forums and councils in every province and across many educational sectors.

A new National Plan for Higher Education calls on the country's thirty-six universities and *tecknikons* (technical universities) actively to recruit non-traditional and adult learners into the system; this is aimed both at opening up tertiary opportunities for the previously disadvantaged, the poor and the marginalized, and at swelling the pool from which institutions can recruit in a national drive to develop the country's human resources and tackle its critical skills shortage.

There is no doubt that South Africa has a firm policy framework that charts a way forward for education and moves the country irrevocably away from apartheid which, as is well known, was characterized by discriminatory, racist and sexist policies, by fragmentation and by irrelevant educational provision for the great majority of the population.

These are great achievements. But in South Africa we have learned to temper our euphoria about the transition and replace it with grim understanding of the enormity of the tasks of reform: we underestimated the problems we now face.

South Africa remains an unequal society. Levels of unemployment are startling and growing: using a broad definition of unemployment, a third of potential workers do not have a job. Youth unemployment is around 50 per cent. School repetition rates are high and many – in some cases most – schools lack basic facilities such as toilets, electricity, water, libraries, stationery and textbooks. These fundamental problems affect the nature of transition negatively six years after the onset of democratic government.

During the 1990s, education was racked by painful and debilitating conflicts over the relationship between the government and constituencies who receive education, and between the government and educators. National government decided that a key strategy in reducing its budget deficits was to reduce the size of the public sector – a familiar move to anybody who knows about structural adjustment programmes.

The largest sector of the public service in South Africa is its teaching force, so for several years the country's educational bureaucracy had to concentrate its energies on resolving conflicts with, and the anxieties of, the educative core. In downsizing the teaching force, and in equalizing teacher/learner ratios between formerly privileged and disadvantaged schools in an effort to reduce glaring funding disparities between them, tens of thousands of teachers were made redundant or took voluntary severance at the same time as South Africa was bringing hundreds of thousands more children into a compulsory school system.

There has been a reduction in real terms in South African educational spending, despite education being a priority area for the new government. In the 2000–01 financial year, however, education consumed 21 per cent of the national budget, with a 6.5 per cent increase stemming the funding decline.

Some conclusions

What conclusions can be drawn from this brief exposition? What can seriously contradictory transitionary processes be attributed to? I would like to suggest that these contradictions also constitute a serious threat to the long-term, visionary goals set out in South African policy documents. Our policies read like poetry and our national leadership aspires to visionary goals. But we have been hit by several very serious problems.

The first problem, which George Papadopoulos and others have referred to, is the extraordinary imperative of economic determinism in the language of our education and training goals. Scarcely a day passes without educators being blamed for being dysfunctional to the economic system, and for failing to produce the automatons who would improve the productivity of our economy, make us global players and advance our capabilities in every sector of economic activity, not social, economic and cultural activity, merely economic activity. Scarcely a day passes without education being accused of failing to discharge its responsibility as a panacea for the problems of the labour market and the problems of unemployment.

Education expenditure is regarded as excessive, badly managed and inefficient, not sufficiently driven by the performance outcomes and audits that are associated with the narrow quantitative measures by which performance is gauged. The kinds of quantitative measures developed over the past twenty-five years by major international policy institutions continue to dominate the discourse of educational efficiency and effectiveness: the cost-benefit analyses and input-output models that speak very little about the sociological questions that drive educational policy change.

A second, associated problem is rapidly declining emphasis on the broader and humanistic goals of education, especially in terms of the struggle for democracy. I raise this not because democracy is an end in itself, but because, taken together, extraordinary economic determinism and the failure to recognize the totality of the values that education must transmit, are going to lead our society into duality once again. They are going to set us firmly on the path of exclusionary policies because the weaker the nature of democracy in our society, the greater the likelihood that large sections of the poor will continue to be left out of the process of change.

A third problem is the reduction of questions about educational expenditure to the prescriptive requirements of particular fiscal targets. There is considerable disquiet in South Africa about how our fiscal targets were arrived at. What covenants with donor or lender agencies drove our fiscal targets? How were they set at particular levels and what measuring instruments were used?

The effect, in the province where I was formerly responsible for administration and policy, was that out of an education budget of nearly 6 billion rands, we were left with just 28 million rands after personnel expenditure. Not a single school could be built and text-books were out of the question. Children were denied fundamental rights guaranteed in our constitution. It is amazing that non-delivery of constitutional rights was not challenged in court: had it been, South Africa's government would have been in serious trouble.

A fourth problem is that the search for international respectability and the imperatives of external pressure on our macro-economic and fiscal policies have intimidated the nation-state into reticence regarding its power and national responsibilities. One of the most profound impacts of globalization is its impact on the behaviour of nation-states. Globalization threatens to paralyse the state in regard to its critical responsibilities to intervene against market and other failures.

All of this is exacerbated, on one hand, by a decline in the effectiveness of democratic organizations and, on the other hand, the rise of powerful conglomerate interests intent on protecting past privileges. The effects of these processes is that we are on the road to a dual system once again, in which we continue to be hostage to the untrammelled effects of particular aspects of globalization.

In conclusion, there are limits to what can be done within any particular country by interventions that are focused on education and training. It is not enough to have good education and training policies. They cannot alone alter the relationship between education and broader policies, because educational policies are merely one expression of the behaviour of the nation-state.

The solutions to the problems that transitional societies such as South Africa face are not national in character. Nations can contribute to resolving their problems by particular forms of contestation and struggles to democratize the way in which resources are used, among other things. But international agencies that are deeply committed to democracy and social justice, such as UNESCO, are a potentially strong bulwark against the predatory instincts of the powerful interests that determine the fate of nations. International agencies and their interventions, linked to critical national responses, might be the only way to hold back the tide of oppressive global division.

9. Open and distance learning in India: critical challenges

Abdul W. Khan
Former Vice-chancellor
of the Indira Gandhi
National Open University
in New Delhi, India.
Now Assistant Director-General
for Communication and
Information at UNESCO

The link between education and development has created what amounts to a 'learning imperative' facing both advanced and developing countries. Bacon's declaration that 'knowledge is power' was more prophetic than factual at the time, but it is certainly valid today. However, knowledge is power only when it is relevant and useful to society.

Takeushi, a Japanese philosopher, said: 'If knowledge is the engine of development, then learning must be its fuel.' Knowledge truly is the engine of development – and it is becoming increasingly central to the development of communities and societies in view of current trends characterized by globalization, liberalization of economies, the pervasive influence of science and technology in our daily lives, and the convergence of communication and information technologies enabling the generation, storage and dissemination of knowledge.

If we accept that knowledge is the engine of development and learning is its fuel, it is not difficult to conclude that we need an adequate supply of fuel to keep the engine running. Front-ended education, which has been the dominant mode of acquiring knowledge, must give way to learning throughout life. Open and distance learning emerged as one of the most important educational innovations of the twentieth century. This chapter looks at its role in meeting critical challenges in lifelong learning.

Responding to critical challenges

The vision of universal education has been constrained by six major challenges: access, quality, cost, equity, relevance, and lack of recognition and opportunities for lifelong learning. Open and distance learning arose as an educational innovation primarily in response to these critical challenges.

Access in open and distance learning systems can be delineated in terms of a range of criteria. The major criteria include:

- The reach of educational provision, especially in terms of patterns of use of information and communication technologies for synchronous-contiguous and asynchronous-non-contiguous dialogue between teachers and learners.
- The degree of response to varied learner needs for a broad range of courses across a spectrum of areas and levels, ranging from awareness through to technical, vocational and professional course offerings.
- The degree of learner autonomy in selecting courses and course combinations from those offered by one or more open and distance learning institutions.
- The degree of flexibility in admission and evaluation procedures, particularly with respect to the relaxation of entry level qualifications, 'on demand' provisions for admitting learners and evaluation of learner performance.
- The use of student support services, especially counselling support available at study centres, work centres and programme centres.
- Trends in enrolments of learners.

The quality of educational products and services is a critical factor determining the impact of educational provision on learners. The challenge of reaching out to an expanded audience must not be seen as distinct from the challenge of providing good-quality learning resources and creating suitable organizational mechanisms. Some of the dimensions of quality education provision by open and distance learning systems are: (a) exposure to a variety of learning resources appealing to multiple senses; (b) creating learning resources that draw on a wide range of expertise in the field; (c) continually updating the knowledge base incorporated in learning resources; (d) adequate and efficient organizational structures; and (e) the delineation of, and adherence to, quality standards for programmes, support services, feedback and evaluation.

All educational institutions need to face up to the challenge of providing quality education to the largest possible number of students at reasonable cost. Both learners and education providers incur costs. In the case of learners, there are monetary costs such as programme fees and the incidental costs entailed in completing programmes, and social opportunity costs in terms of time and effort. In the case of education providers, cost effectiveness has been calculated in terms of cost-recovery rates for institutions, for operations such as admission, counselling and evaluation, and for programmes and courses.

The issue of equity is central to the philosophy of open and distance learning and requires close examination of total enrolment figures and disaggregated enrolment data for disadvantaged population groups. Trends in enrolment also need careful analysis. Bridging the urban–rural–tribal divide, the gender divide and the class divide is crucial to meeting the challenge of equity. Combating disadvantage could be considered one of the major planks of open and distance learning. Providing education to the disadvantaged needs to be seen not only in terms of gaining access to the system, but also in terms of accessing relevant education.

Relevance is a challenge for the general population of learners as well. To meet it, appropriate systems that are responsive to techno-logical and socio-economic structures must emerge.

Traditionally, educational provision has been front-ended and limited to young learners seeking basic and professional qualifications. But open and distance learning institutions are by nature 'open' to learners of all ages and backgrounds. They therefore address issues of *lifelong learning* beyond the usual educational span. Creating appro-priate inputs for lifelong learning is a major concern for open and distance learning.

Unique features of open and distance learning

Open and distance learning is characterized by the transmission of educational or instructional programmes to geographically dispersed individuals and groups. This asynchronous dialogue between teacher and learner occurs between individuals separated in space and/or time. The asynchronous and non-contiguous nature of the learning process is central to the philosophy of openness in open and distance learning. The instructional system (Figure 1) confers on the educational process learner centricity and learner autonomy, and substantially contributes to ease of access to open and distance learning.

Fig. 1. The instructional system in open and distance learning institutions

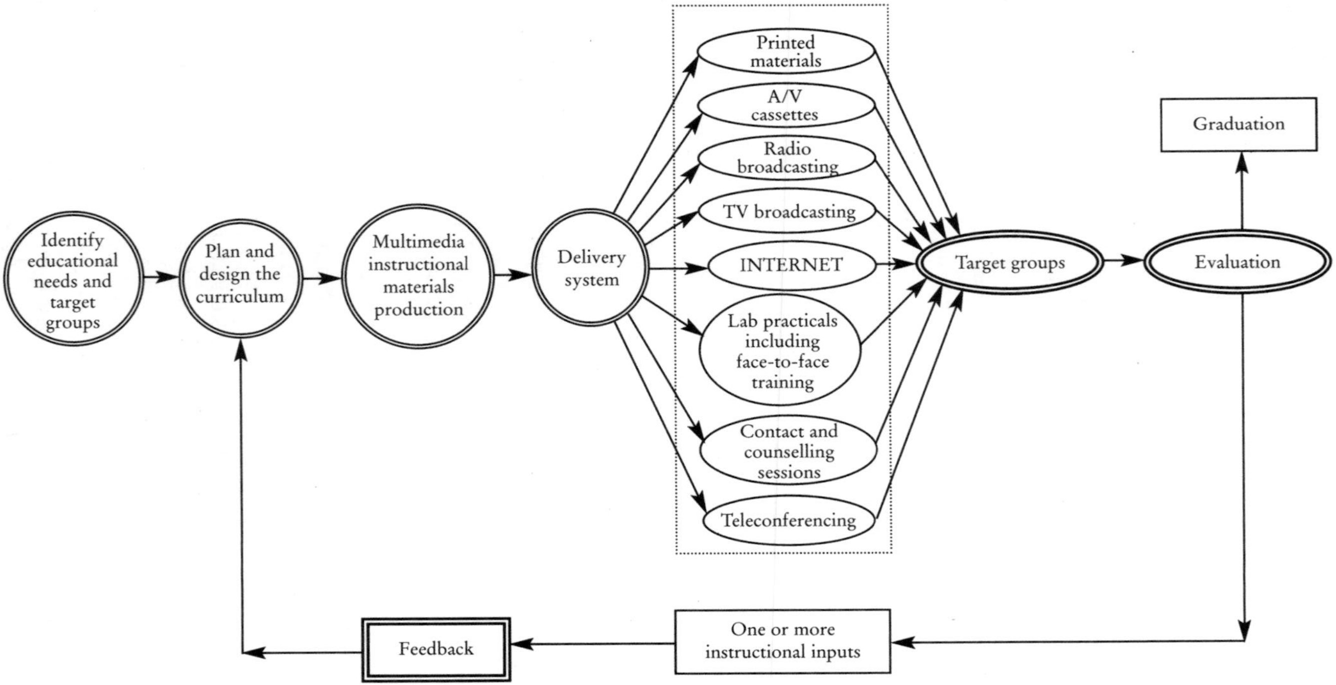

Depending on the degree of openness of an institution, learners may also be offered the option to choose from wide course offerings and course combinations drawn from various disciplines. Mobility of learners from one distance education institution to another through appropriate credit-transfer mechanisms also contributes to learner autonomy.

The philosophy of openness also permeates the creation of appropriate institutional structures and mechanisms for delivering instructional inputs. Programme delivery by open and distance learning institutions emphasizes delivery through multiple channels (Figure 2). Multi-channel delivery includes three types of inputs: direct to learner, through resource centres and through extension activities.

Fig. 2. Instructional inputs and channels of delivery modes

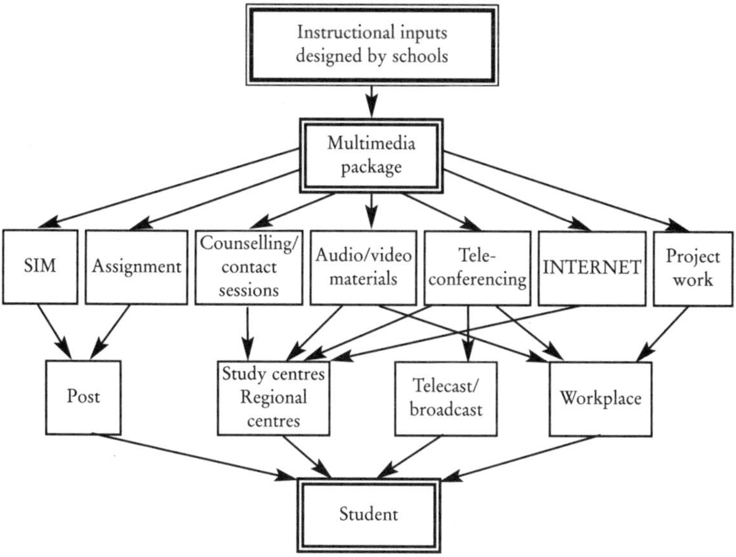

Delivery direct to learners includes inputs such as print, audiovisual cassettes, broadcast programmes, on-line computer networks and distance-learning facilitators (or mentors or co-ordinators). Resource centres catering to the needs of learners cover a broad canvas and include study centres, work centres, partner institutions, multimedia learning centres and local institutions or organizations providing delivery of services. Extension activities of open and distance learning institutions generally involve co-operation with governmental and non-governmental organizations.

The use of modern information and communication technologies (ICTs) is inseparable from open and distance learning. Global trends in the use of ICTs include: (a) convergence – of telecommunications, television and computers through digitization and compression techniques; (b) miniaturization; (c) increased mobility, for example wireless; (d) enhanced processing chips; (e) more powerful and user-friendly commands and software tools; and (f) reduced costs.

ICTs play a crucial role in open and distance learning. Their use overcomes socio-economic barriers, reduces the communication gap, enhances virtual proximity and provides greater access, offers a greater variety of learning resources, enables individualized learning, enhances interactivity, provides more powerful cognitive tools, enables greater learner control and provides greater flexibility.

The selection of appropriate ICTs and their effective use are critical issues for open and distance learning institutions. The dimensions that govern the appropriateness of a given technology include: accessibility, compatibility with local infrastructure, financial and human resources, user friendliness and maintenance support. The effective use of ICTs by open and distance learning systems has been characterized by a multimedia approach, integration of technology, training and sustainability.

These methodological and technological features are major contributors to the uniqueness of open and distance learning systems, and are responsible for their phenomenal growth. Some other reasons for growth include demographic, economic, social and political factors. At a broader level, these factors contribute to the two major 'engines' driving the process of change and the growth and consolidation of open and distance learning systems – growing demand for knowledge and skills development, and convergence of information and communication technologies.

The current trends in growth and diversity of open and distance learning systems include expansion in numbers and types of learners, variety of distance education providers, increased breadth of operations (settings and purposes for which they are used), diversity in applications (non-formal education, technical and vocational, agriculture), diversification of delivery mechanisms, shift from the use of a single medium through multiple media to multimedia, use of a variety of learning resources, greater emphasis on interactive technologies, increased stress on the application of open and distance learning in training, growing emphasis on extension activities, single institutions to dual mode and multimode institutions, and greater stress on collaborative and consortium based approaches with internal and external agencies.

Some case-studies of learning throughout life

Awareness building

Certificate programme in food and nutrition
The certificate programme was designed to build awareness of the role of food in ensuring healthy living for the individual, the family and community. The content focused on selected key areas: nutrients and their functions; food preparation and processing; utilization of food by the body; and the economics of food production and distribution. The target audience consists primarily of women with basic but limited formal education.

The course content, treatment and media mix were developed keeping the learning competences of the target group in mind. Practical components were incorporated as home-based activities interwoven with the printed text. The programme is offered in eleven languages to cater to regional audiences, and especially to older women who are only familiar with their regional language. The programme has attracted a fair number of older women, who have brought their rich and varied life experience to the learning process.

The core medium used consists of printed booklets supported by supplementary audio and video inputs. The audio and video components are accessible to learners at study centres. Transmission of video programmes dubbed in the regional language through local cable television networks has been successfully attempted in certain states in India.

Counselling support builds on experience-sharing and problem solving. Counsellors have observed that learners often need to overcome their initial diffidence, some because they are returning to a formal learning situation after several years' absence. Special attention has been focused on developing study skills in the distance-learning context. The transition to individualized learning remains a gradual process for many learners; counselling and group interaction have therefore been increasingly stressed in the instructional sequence.

Technical and vocational skills development

Construction workers' vocational qualification project
This project was designed and launched in collaboration with the Construction Industry Development Council. Certificate programmes for construction workers are on offer at the trade and supervisory development levels. At the trade-skill level, courses relate to masonry, bar-bending and shuttering carpentry. At the supervisory development level, they concern general works supervision.

Tannery workers' vocational qualification project
Certificate programmes for tannery workers, also at trade and supervisory development levels, were launched in collaboration with the Central Leather Research Institute. The trade courses cater to soak-yard workers, dehairing workers, lime-yard workers, drum-yard workers, fleshers, scudders and splitters. The supervisory courses help meet the skills needs of supervisors in soak-yards, lime-yards, machine-yards and drum-yards.

The target audience for both projects is functionally literate. The focus is on upgrading skills and improving work performance. Entry to the programmes is granted on the basis of prior achievement or work experience. Learners are expected to achieve performance standards laid down by the industry. The learning materials include print material and audio cassettes using a step-by-step approach, with reasons given for adopting particular techniques.

Counselling support is provided at the tannery site itself by supervisory staff. Staff drawn from industry help the tanneries in filling out forms and completing the requirements of the university. Evaluation of learner performance is carried out by work inspectors, also from the industry.

Training local self-government functionaries

Panchayati Raj Project
Panchayats are village-level councils. With growing devolution of power to local authorities, there was great need for capacity-building

among more than 3 million *panchayat* members across the country. Support for the project was provided by the Ministry of Rural Areas and Employment. Training is expected to result in improved competence on the part of elected members as regards fostering socio-economic transformation of communities.

Self-learning material is supplemented by audio and video programmes. Since the audience is composed of new literates, the focus is on simple presentation and extensive illustration. By early 1999, the programme had covered about 58,000 elected *panchayat* members in four districts of one state. Audio and video packages have been used for publicity campaigns, especially during local events such as village fairs and markets. An effort is being made to cater to illiterate learners as well, through special televison lessons based on the self-learning print material.

The cascade model of training has been adopted, with the university faculty directly training master trainers who, in turn, train local counsellors to conduct contact programmes at the village level. Creating a cadre of trained local counsellors has been a major focal point of the strategy. To cater to *panchayat* members in other states, the self-learning print material is being translated into major regional languages. The video cassettes are being dubbed in regional languages as well.

Conclusion

It is widely recognized that front-ended education cannot meet learning requirements in the face of rapid societal and technological change. The need for lifelong learning, therefore, is firmly established. Open and distance learning are among the methods ideally suited to cater to lifelong-learning imperatives. Their unique features make them particularly responsive to educational challenges.

The Indira Gandhi National Open University is one of the largest open and distance-learning institutions in the world. The university recognized the need to go beyond formal and professional education, and has given special attention to meeting the differing needs for lifelong learning of diverse communities. The case-studies highlight the university's experiences in promoting learning throughout life.

Conclusion

Jacques Delors
Chair of the International Commission
on Education for the Twenty-first Century,
UNESCO

The 1996 report of UNESCO's International Commission on Education for the Twenty-first Century, *Learning: The Treasure Within*, has been published in about thirty languages and editions. So it is pertinent to ask whether it is the report that appeals or the subject. During his election campaign, British Prime Minister Tony Blair described his top three priorities as 'education, education and education'. It thus appears that the subject itself is important, not only for experts but also for policy makers, businesses, trade unions and voluntary organizations. Education has become a hot topic in a fast moving world.

Many doubtless believe that politicians talk about learning throughout life because it is the 'in' thing to do. We must be wary of fashion, because it can destroy an idea before it is put into practice – particularly at a time like this, when people and governments are still feeling their way around the ideas and issues involved in lifelong learning.

A desire to take forward concepts of lifelong learning led Roberto Carneiro and Alexandra Draxler to select the subjects covered in the chapters of this book. Their aim was not to present a bird's eye view of the subject, but to head straight for milestones on the road to lifelong learning, and to take a look at informal sectors of education that hold new prospects, examples and paths that may be helpful in the future.

Although our Commission, which draws members from every

continent, had some difficulty in reconciling different conceptions of humanity on earth and in history – to put it simplistically, Western, Eastern and other conceptions – we would be wrong to consider lifelong learning a necessity for rich countries and a luxury for poor ones. Less developed countries stress the importance of this theme. But learning throughout life is relevant to all of our societies, for many good reasons, and representatives of developing countries recognize the need for and importance of the concept.

The idea of this report was not to produce *Learning: The Treasure Within* all over again, but with the help of eminent specialists from around the world to discover cornerstones that will help guide us to a new education. We must learn lessons from those who are active outside the strictly formal sector, who can show us innovative aspects of successful experiments and can demonstrate what has achieved progress in education, contributed to the fight against unequal opportunity and overcome obstacles of distance, poverty and lack of resources.

In other words we must concentrate on learning, from people working outside the formal sector, to pass on to the young and not so young what humanity has learned about itself – against a backdrop in which the media is forcing us to live without memories, in a climate of instant reaction and emotional excitement. Such humanitarian learning is reassuring, and helps us understand a diversity of situations.

The four pillars of education

The most striking aspect of *Learning: The Treasure Within* was the four pillars of education (not wisdom) it identified – Learning to Know, Learning to Do, Learning to Live Together and Learning to Be.

The first two concepts have long been self-evident pillars of education. Learning to Be was advocated in the 1972 UNESCO report of the same name, which flowed from its International Commission on the Development of Education chaired by the celebrated politician Edgar Faure. It was an era of student revolts, the end of the 'Golden Sixties' for Europe and a time of trouble, too, in the United States, when people wanted to shrug off constraints and be free of the tyranny of growth. Some even called for zero growth. How wrong they were!

Learning: The Treasure Within retained Learning to Be because education still fundamentally aims to show people how to achieve better self knowledge and fulfilment. The idea is not just to label people by their abilities in different disciplines, but also to take account of their active participation in school, working and daily life. People must be able to express what they feel: this would not be possible if, right from the start and throughout life, education systems were to exclude whole sets of high-quality talents. This means nothing less than a revolution in education that will be expensive in terms of time.

More specifically in keeping with today – and with UNESCO's tireless striving for peace, which should be acknowledged – is Learning to Live Together. This newer pillar has a special resonance in the twenty-first century as countries grapple with the difficulties of co-existence among different religious communities, different ethnic groups and others.

Education bears a tremendous responsibility to bring to blossom all the seeds within every individual, and to make communication between people easier. Communication does not simply mean repeating what we have learned: it also means also articulating what is in us and has been combined into a rounded whole through education, and understanding others.

Combining the four pillars, it should be emphasized, is especially important today when many economies are booming, are dominating political decisions and are tending to impose their requirements on education systems. The dominance of economics has, needless to say, led to a revolt by arts and humanities teachers who believe that mastery of language and all its riches, and an ability to express oneself clearly, are essential to conducting a dialogue with others and communicating thinking.

Together the four pillars provide balance at a time when many policy makers still speak of education only in terms of the economy and labour market. It is laudable to try to combat social exclusion and poverty by helping everybody to access society through work (provided that work exists). But we must not overlook the other aspect of education – the personal and collective dimension – through which people are empowered to achieve self-mastery. It is not possible to cope with life's ups and downs without confidence in ourselves and some control over our destiny. Reconciling the four pillars is not easy, but their co-existence in *Learning: The Treasure Within* reminds everybody concerned with education of their full duty.

After establishing the pillars, the Commission concentrated on three key issues that have been the subject of follow-up.

The first is the importance of basic education in all countries. Again the United Kingdom raised this issue following investigations that would have led to the same outcome had they been conducted elsewhere in Europe: between the ages of 11 and 15 years, the number of young people without a grasp of basic skills is tragically high – some cannot read, write, calculate or express themselves adequately. Another example is the European car industry where workers over 40 years, equipped with what they learned at school, are incapable of adapting to new forms of labour organization. These are tasks of good basic education, without which it is pointless to talk about lifelong learning, even in industrialized societies.

The second issue is the need to diversify secondary education, and the third is widening the tasks of higher education, particularly universities, whose key objective is to restore intellect to the place it has lost in contemporary society to those arbiters of taste, the media.

Learning amidst tensions and change

Learning: The Treasure Within identified several tensions to be found amidst learning imperatives. There are three that are worth reiterating here.

The first is between the universal and the individual. In Asian countries, depending on the religion or culture, individuals are just part of the 'background' and the universal takes precedence. Those beliefs do not have the same resonance in Europe. The individual dimension represents the part of education that should enable each of us to know ourselves better, to develop and to control our own destinies. In some countries, this tension also represents resistance to the cultural trivialization that globalization can bring. In India, for instance, some intellectuals argue that their country should defend itself not only against Coca-Cola and McDonald's but also against a globalized culture, a 'reach-me-down' way of thinking universally applied. It is no simple matter for educators to resolve such issues.

The second tension is between tradition and modernity. This is a twofold issue that has not just arisen at the dawn of the twenty-first century. Modernity has been significant since the Enlightenment. How were societies, bogged down as they were in traditions, customs and ways of living, able to embrace modernity – and what exactly is modernity? These are awesome questions. Then there is the trivial use of the word 'modernize', which is so commonly used (especially by politicians) that it no longer means anything: we must 'modernize' the economy and labour market, education and social relationships. It is a broad and confusing theme that educators can no longer see beyond. Today, modernity raises the question: are we giving birth to a new world with very strong demands that will compel us to resolve the awkward dichotomy between tradition and modernity?

Finally, there is tension between the spiritual and the temporal. Colleagues from Asia argued forcefully in the Commission that youth's thirst for an ideal must be satisfied, and education systems must foster a quest for meaning and values. This was said without questioning the need for philosophical and spiritual pluralism, but many Commission members feared that under cover of neutrality it is possible to neglect people's spiritual values, to fail to respect them and even to cease knowing what they are. Put another way, neutrality is not just passivity but active pluralism and exchange. Resolving this tension is the responsibility of teachers and institutions where young people are taught. For this reason, the Commission emphasized teaching history and, to achieve better mutual understanding worldwide, the history of religions as part of civics: in many countries, civic education includes learning about religions.

These are tensions that educators in earlier centuries might have confronted, albeit in different contexts. What is new about them that must be taken into account?

First, the tension between the global and local – a phenomenon that is not purely educational and societal in nature – brings with it risks of breakdown of social ties, with accompanying changes in lifestyles such as the separation of couples and great economic transformation. Globalization on the march is making contemporary societies dizzy. Most businesses already think globally, and when employees are told that the company is compelled to dismiss them, often the reason cited is globalization, or competition. For the average person, globalization thus seems quite threatening: it is perceived as a machine for destroying jobs and upsetting lifestyles, because most people think in local terms. Tensions between the global and local also explain democratic malaise – the difficulties advanced democracies face in maintaining active citizenship.

Another new aspect of global–local tension is that while on the one hand there is globalization – with multinational firms, internationally mobile young people and images that reach us instantaneously from the far corners of the globe – on the other hand there is fragmentation, with more nation-states than there were thirty years ago, ethnic tensions and minority drives for self-determination the world over. This is an issue beyond the educator's task, but one that must be stressed with seriousness and insistence, since fragmentation does not occur in peaceful isolation but brings tensions, destabilization and civil war. Young people at school must be made aware of this tension. They must learn that the zero risk society does not exist, and that contrary to the writing of Francis Fukuyama in *The End of History and the Last Man* (1992), the end of the Cold War and communism has not ushered in universal peace, democracy or pluralism. The world faces many risks, and fragmentation is one of them.

A second, much debated aspect of change are dangers inherent in the breakdown of social structures and rampant individualism. Much writing in the United States and Europe is based on the principle that we live in the age of the individual. Some argue that there is nothing new about this: that since the Enlightenment the emphasis has been on the individual rather than on society, in order to free people from over-constrictive communal straitjackets.

But excessive individualism raises moral issues and poses problems for society. Who feels solidarity with whom? The philosophy of the market economy and society raises this question: the individual is regarded as a rational *Homo economicus*, and following in the footsteps of philosopher and economist Hayek, it is argued that we should be pleased that individuals are able to control their destinies and that the only links they establish are those they consider useful or interesting.

Individualism is reflected in other factors, such as changing lifestyles and consumption patterns. The proportion of working women in industrial societies is growing, which greatly alters family life and even concepts of the family and social organization. Rapid urbanization and the uncontrolled expansion of cities are other aspects of change, applying especially to Africa, South America and Asia, which are creating administrative problems and districts that are characterized by social exclusion and poverty, with their many attendant problems.

We can therefore argue that a great communal vacuum has been created and must be filled if the groundwork for a new relationship between individuals and their communities is to be laid. There are pressing problems that are peculiar to our time, but social breakdown is not new: more than a century ago sociologist Emile Durkheim spoke of the essential similarities of community life, but even then said that the similarities, and living together, were crumbling. Similarly, Benjamin Constant said with extreme scepticism, foreshadowing the philosophy of Raymond Aron: 'Nearly all the pleasures of the moderns are private in their existence. The vast majority are always excluded from power and necessarily attach only a very passing interest to its public existence.'

Learning and the new economy

Many societies today stress the relationship between education and jobs, and this raises three fundamental questions. Capitalism has spread across the globe while communism has ceased to exist in all but a few countries – but will there be one capitalism in future, or more than one? The second question is about the market and regulation: is everything to be subject to the market or must there be regulation and, if so, what sort of regulation? A third question pertains to the centrality of work, bearing in mind that for the past fifteen years we have been bombarded by publications announcing the end of work.

Capitalism or 'capitalisms'?

Globalization is upsetting the balance of power, the global financial market being the most striking illustration. Globalization is characterized by the interdependence of economies and the welcome rise of many developing countries, which have become global competitors. But after the Asian economic crisis of 1998, even fervent supporters of the market queried a capitalist framework that allows global economic disaster. While economists studied economic indicators, the real issue was millions of people thrown out of work and into poverty – the crisis was paid for by poverty and exclusion. The market does not necessarily lead to exclusion, but there are problems, which is why many people are wondering whether institutions such as the International Monetary Fund and World Bank should be reformed.

It is widely contended that globalization will lead to cultural and social uniformity. There are arguments for defending creative local people against invasion by a formidable American cinema and media industry, for instance, but we should not complain about the imposition of uniformity and do nothing. The weight of tradition is still heavy: in the cinema industry, where American films account for 80 per cent of box office takings even in Europe, creative individuals are none the less emerging in a number of countries, including the United Kingdom and France.

Also, even in the opinion of market economists, the nation remains an important player in the battle for economic prosperity and social progress. Californian professor Manuel Castel explains clearly how nations are on the side of their businesses in waging the battle for competitiveness. One justification for European integration is that European countries have to join forces to retain an enviable place in tomorrow's world and not become marginalized.

It appears, therefore, that even in a globalizing world dominated by capitalism there are counter-balances to an intervention in the global market.

The market *versus* regulation

The second question flows from the first. The market is playing a more important role than in the past, but the issue is whether we have absolute confidence in the 'invisible hand' and the doctrine of individualism. These were ideas behind the Thatcherite revolution of the 1980s. When former British Prime Minister Margaret Thatcher was asked to hold discussions with 'social partners' – employers and trade unions – she famously replied that there was no such thing as society, just individuals. There are markets and individuals, and a doctrinal conflict between neo-liberals and neo-Keynesians.[1] At issue is the absence of discipline, and of a minimum number of global rules. This trend has also brought fresh conflicts between capital and labour, with the balance of power tilting against trade unions and workers.

We thus have two sets of data to reconcile. The first is the battle for competitiveness, which cannot be ignored – including in the education of children. If schools reject an environment of competitiveness, they will raise weak individuals unable to hold their own in life and attain self-fulfilment. Second, theories of growth must be based on relationships between technological progress, business potential and the capacities of public institutions. To return to Manuel Castel, reconciliation is based on a combination of reduced costs, increased productivity, expanded markets and speeded-up capital rotation. Therefore,

---

1. Not those who advocate a budget deficit in order to create jobs, but those who consider that regulatory institutions are needed.

we are talking again about the organization of work with the participation of all parties concerned, the right to lifelong learning and the collective research-and-development effort.

The end of work?

The third area in which the economy challenges the educator is that of work, which still occupies a central position in societies. People who access work access society: those outside work do not. Denmark, with a population of just over 5 million people, faced the danger of having 600,000 inhabitants with no work experience, dependent on insurance schemes and/or state welfare – something its Social Democrat government has tried to end.

The individualization of work, which is producing fragmented societies, characterizes today's economies thanks to knowledge disseminated through information processing, the development of service activities and the growing importance of information- and knowledge-based professions. This future must be viewed frankly and fearlessly. For example, most economic analyses are still based on surveys of industry, but that sector now accounts for only 30 to 35 per cent of GNP in industrialized nations. Not surprisingly, industrialists are being defeatist at a time when the service sector is growing: but this does not reflect feeling throughout economies. Intellectual transformation is needed, even in teaching basic economics.

What will the consequences of new working environments be? One will undoubtedly be greater autonomy for certain categories of workers. But for young people autonomy will have to come from education: it will not occur spontaneously. There will also be organization into networks of businesses and of workers. If spontaneous evolution continues there will be increased inequality of income. Technological development is occurring at the expense of unskilled workers, which explains why emphasis is being placed on 'skilling' young people and on the long-term unemployed in every European country, especially the United Kingdom. There are three reasons why Rifkin's 'end of work' forecast will not come true.

First, while increased demand does not offset increased work productivity, a reduction in working time does. Just after the Second World War, a worker lucky enough to be employed throughout life spent 100,000 hours at work in all. This has been reduced to 70,000 hours at work, and some predict that this figure will be 45,000 hours in thirty years' time. This raises issues of how to organize non-working time and educating people to make the best use of it.

Second, recent innovations explain unemployment, reduction in working hours and the spontaneous, massive decrease in working time connected with processes – to 'how to produce'. But current innovation is also directed at 'what to produce'. New outlets are therefore appearing which could need workers to exploit them.

Furthermore, changes in family structures, the entry of women into the labour market and urbanization are creating new needs. In the United States, for instance, services to individuals and communities account for 40 per cent of jobs. We are facing a situation accurately described by Robert Reich in *The Work of Nations: Preparing Ourselves for 21st Century Capitalism.* He writes that in future there will be three categories of worker: the manipulators of symbols, the winners in a globalized economy with a high technological content; workers in routine jobs, who will be the main losers because they will be in direct competition with low-wage countries and machines; and increasing numbers of service providers.

Milestones on the road to lifelong learning

This rather crude classification is very revealing of what society expects of education from the point of view of future preparation for work – the milestones on the road to learning throughout life.

First there is the relationship between human beings and information technology. This is the heart of the matter, with its requirements regarding production structures, work organization, and the world of leisure and culture. All this is developing extraordinary opportunities for access to information and knowledge. The Commission did not tackle this task for lack of the proper qualifications. There are as yet no overall assessments of the political, economic and social consequences of the information society.

Some argue that information technologies are an excellent development, reducing factory work and giving employees greater control over the product quality of their work: they ask why similar principles should not apply to teachers. The Commission disagreed with this, the reason being that teachers do not just oversee a relationship in which knowledge is passed on but also have a personal relationship with learners. Teachers try to awaken qualities that lie within learners and to impart a corpus of acquired knowledge, such that the combination of what is innate and what is learned enables them to get along in life. Together with the new information technologies, the teacher/taught or teacher/learner relationship thus remains one of the fundamental problems of education, something that has not changed since Aristotle.

Second, there is the relationship between society and the education system. In France, when something goes wrong it is always the school's fault. We do not blame parents or society or the media, which argues that society should be zero-risk (whenever a climbing accident or traffic jam occurs, journalists call up the minister to ask what he or she is doing about it). In the media, children learn that society is supposed to be zero-risk, but it is not. Who will teach children to confront risks, if not the school? Yet we cannot ask the school to do everything. The Commission took great interest in countries in which schools are an integral part of the local setting: in which whole communities, not just parents and pupils, are involved.

The third milestone – equal opportunity – remains one of the fundamental goals of education. Leaving behind the perennial debate, in which conservatives feel that what matters is the innate and that nothing much is added by learning, the school can make a contribution (over and above the innate) to enabling everyone to acquire the building blocks of life. This has been made all the more difficult because of the mass expansion of secondary and higher education with its considerable wastage, enormous frustrations and high costs. Faced with this expansion and extension of education, some are questioning whether equality can be reconciled with quality – a question that haunted the Commission.

The main question, however, lies elsewhere and concerns the diversity of paths along which all young people can access knowledge, society and work. For this reason, the Commission proposed education vouchers: young people not wanting to continue their studies, deciding instead to enter the labour market, would receive vouchers enabling them to return to school or university later under a continuing education or lifelong-learning scheme. But how ought we to manage the transition from adult education to lifelong learning, especially when studies show that after twenty-five years the biggest beneficiaries of continuing education are those who are already the most highly educated? This is why we decided to review adult education, including worker and informal education, in the work we will do to follow up this report.

How can we make the transition to lifelong learning, which implies changing formal education systems and ending the division between initial and adult education in favour of a continuous learning process, but which cannot be achieved without the participation of other actors in society – policy makers, business, the voluntary sector and trade unions?

Nobody knows exactly how to proceed. But in our view, lifelong learning makes it possible to give order to different educational sequences, to manage transitions, to diversify and personalize individual paths and to provide second or third chances.

In achieving comprehensive, quality systems of lifelong learning we would avoid the fatal dilemma posed by conservatives of all shades of opinion, on the right and on the left – either select, albeit with increased risk of exclusion, to ensure excellence and the emergence of an élite, or abandon the idea of excellence and overall education quality, without necessarily avoiding academic failure and frustrations, as twenty years' experience of the *collège unique* in France have shown.

The questions confronting us are formidable. But they must be tackled if we are to travel the road towards learning throughout life – if we are to ensure in future that we unlock, for all, the treasure within.